The 500 Hidden Secrets of

ROTTERDAM

INTRODUCTION

This is a guide to the hidden gems of Rotterdam. It takes you off the beaten track to discover the city's turbulent history, its modern architecture, its little-known museums, the best restaurants and the coolest cocktail bars. You'll also find a lot of places that are worth visiting in the port area. Rotterdam's port is the largest one in Europe – it is said that one in every two soft drinks on the continent pass through it. The port area only recently became a tourist destination, leaving much to be discovered.

The 500 Hidden Secrets of Rotterdam lists the places the authors would recommend to a friend who wanted to discover the real Rotterdam. With this book in your pocket, you can set out to find an old police station where the coffee is served by former troublemakers, or catch a band in the hold of a former light vessel. Or how about discovering a secret beach where sailors in poor health were once kept in quarantine? Rotterdam is also a city of food and drink. It has something for everyone, from Michelin-starred restaurants to the best Surinamese snack bars. Sample some of the local beers or try a cup of locally roasted coffee. The city is famous for the can-do mentality of its inhabitants and for offering plenty of room to experiment. You'll find exciting galleries and art venues, as well as innovative festivals and trendy clubs. Here you can admire the fantastic collection of Museum Boijmans Van Beuningen in a shiny new depot and visit a former garage for cutting-edge art expositions.

HOW TO
USE THIS BOOK?

This book contains 500 things to know about Rotterdam in 100 different categories. Some are places to visit, others are random bits of information. The aim is to inspire, not to cover the city from A to Z.

The places listed in the guide are given an address, a district and a number. The district and number allow you to find the locations on the maps at the beginning of the book. The maps are not detailed enough to navigate around the city, but you can pick up a good city map at the Rotterdam Info desk at the entrance of the Central Station. Check Rotterdam Info online at *rotterdam.info*.

You need to bear in mind that cities change all the time. The chef who hits a high note one day may be uninspiring on the day you happen to visit. The hotel ecstatically reviewed in this book might suddenly go downhill under a new manager. The bar considered one of the 5 best places with a great beer selection might be empty on the night you visit.

This is obviously a highly personal selection. You might not always agree with it. If you want to leave a comment, recommend a bar or reveal your favourite secret place, please visit the website *the500hiddensecrets.com* or follow *@500hiddensecrets* on Instagram or Facebook and leave a comment.

THE AUTHORS

Saskia Naafs and Guido van Eijck are researchers and writers. They specialise in a wide range of topics, from politics and urban planning to education and housing. They are also the authors of *The 500 Hidden Secrets of Amsterdam* and *Hidden Holland*. Both Saskia and Guido were born in Rotterdam and after having moved around quite a few times, decided to return to their home city, drawn by its diverse population, its amazing cultural scene, its beautiful waterfront vistas, and its excellent museums, shops and restaurants.

Saskia suggests exploring the Nieuwe Binnenweg where you can find the best record stores, vintage shops, lunch spots, restaurants and pubs. Walk all the way to the end of this street, and you'll suddenly find yourself in the historic harbour of Delfshaven, from where the Pilgrim Fathers set sail in the 17th century.

Guido recommends spending time in the south of the city. Ride the wooden escalator of the Maastunnel, grab a drink in vibrant Katendrecht, check out a great example of Dutch modernist architecture in the Kiefhoek neighbourhood and visit the multicultural market in Afrikaanderplein. Cross the iconic Erasmus Bridge and marvel at the magnificent view of the river.

The authors wish to thank their friends, family, colleagues and acquaintances for offering invaluable insights about the city. Without their precious help, it would have been impossible to draw up a list of so many places, some of which tourists have never heard of, and some that even born and bred Rotterdammers don't know.

ROTTERDAM

overview

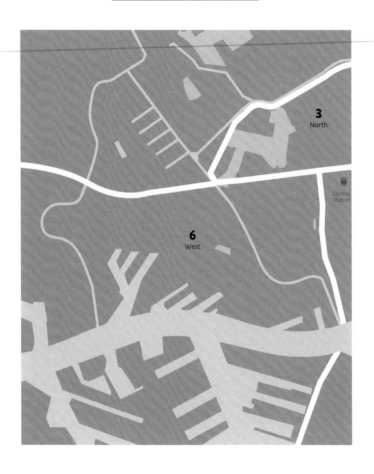

3
North

Central
Station

6
West

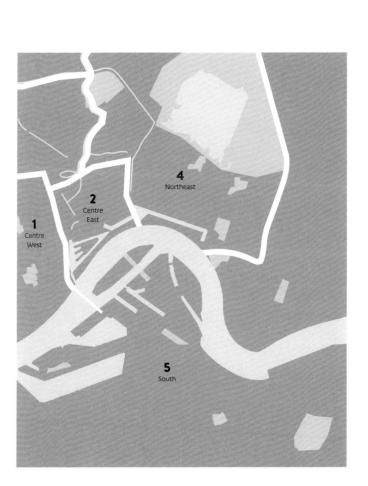

1
Centre
West

2
Centre
East

4
Northeast

5
South

Map 1
CENTRE WEST

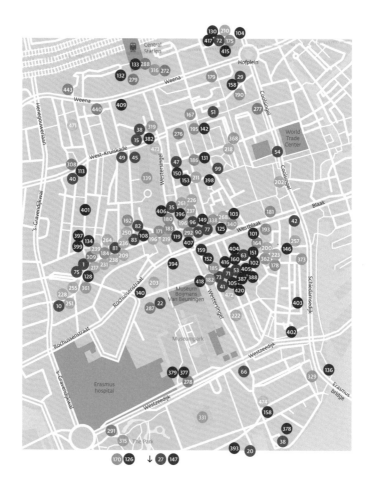

Map 2
CENTRE EAST

Map 3
NORTH

Map 4
NORTHEAST

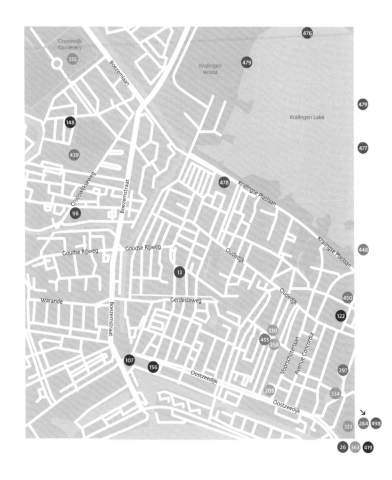

Map 5
SOUTH

Map 6
WEST

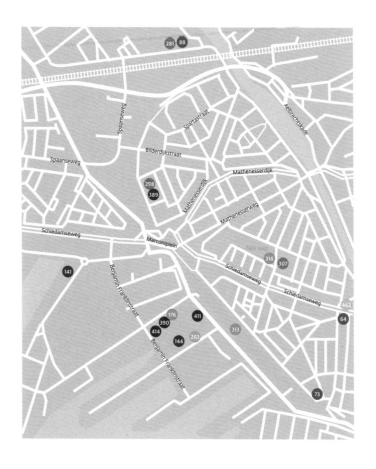

MECCA

100 PLACES
TO EAT TASTY FOOD

The 5 nicest places to go for
BREAKFAST

---

1   LILITH

**Nieuwe Binnen-
weg 125-H
Centre West** ①
+31 (0)10 203 88 38
lilithcoffee.nl

No fuss, no decaf and no reservations. Lilith (run by the sisters Charlotte and Florence Damen) serves a strong cup of coffee and breakfast throughout the day in this blue and black cosy restaurant. The menu features all the classics, from blueberry pancakes to eggs Benedict, from French toast to homemade granola.

2   PICKNICK

**Mariniersweg 259
Centre East** ②
+31 (0)6 148 566 85
picknickrotterdam.nl

Early birds flock to Picknick for a good cup of locally roasted coffee. From 8 am onwards, find yourself a cosy spot at one of the tables for a quick croissant, a superhealthy *açai* berry breakfast, scrambled eggs with chorizo, or go full out and take your time to enjoy the luxurious 'picknick platter'.

3 CAFFE BOOON

Proveniersstraat 31
North ③
+31 (0)10 737 07 82
caffebooon.nl

For anyone who loves strong Italian coffee (served from 8.30 am), Italian cakes, big sandwiches *(tramezzini* and *piadine)* and small delicious pastries. It's tempting to spend the whole day in this lovely light Italian corner oasis, and move effortlessly from breakfast to lunch to a late afternoon snack with a glass of wine.

4 BY JARMUSCH

Goudsesingel 64
Centre East ②
+31 (0)10 307 48 09
byjarmusch.nl

By Jarmusch serves breakfast all day in an American-style diner. Typical American dishes (pancakes, hash browns, steak & eggs) are served with a good 'cup of joe': fresh filter coffee served at your table. The name refers to Jim Jarmusch's film *Coffee and Cigarettes* in which famous actors drink copious amounts of coffee while chatting in a diner.

5 SANDWICH CORNER

Glashaven 2-B
Centre East ②
+31 (0)10 413 58 57
sandwichcorner.nl

For over 30 years, Wim Bloemink has been building a steady fanbase with his crispy fresh bread and superb homemade cold cuts. His grilled sausage is phenomenal, as are the roast beef, spicy chicken, pulled pork and tuna sandwiches. There's also a nice selection of cheese and sweet toppings. The Sandwich Corner is open from 9 am till 4 pm.

The 5 best places for a
HEALTHY LUNCH

6 **DELI TASTY**
Meent 40
Centre East ②
+31 (0)10 411 11 16
delitasty.nl

Vietnamese street food cooked to perfection at affordable prices. Take a seat and enjoy a deliciously soothing *pho* soup on a cold and windy day, or try one of the *bánh mì* sandwiches or fresh salads. Top off your meal with Vietnamese ice coffee. Deli Tasty is a very down-to-earth Asian eatery in an otherwise high-end shopping street.

8 MECCA

7 DE KOK EN DE TUINMAN

Koningsveldestraat 14
North ③
+31 (0)6 528 384 37
dekokendetuinman.com

Chef Ceciel and gardener Anna have created a fantastic garden and restaurant on the site of a former schoolyard, well hidden from the city's hustle and bustle. Settle down here for an organic and locally sourced breakfast, lunch or a fabulous piece of cake (available for takeaway). Open Thursday through Sunday, 9 am - 6 pm.

8 MECCA

Noordsingel 39
North ③
+31 (0)10 737 01 75
meccarotterdam.nl

For the best veggie Middle Eastern food, head over to Mecca, where the pita, falafel and *fattoush* look mouth-watering and taste even better. They serve some very good homemade lemonades and refreshing iced coffees too. Open from 9 to 5 and for Friday night drinks.

9 STATENCAFÉ

Statenweg 134-D
North ③
+31 (0)10 720 16 00
statencafe.com

A classic grand cafe with a great people-watching terrace that serves equally classic lunch fare like a club sandwich and a Caesar salad. Do try the Dutch evergreen: two croquettes served on sliced bread – there's a vegan option too. Located on the corner of beautiful Statensingel, it's also close to the Vroesenpark.

10 THE TEA LAB

Nieuwe Binnen-
weg 178-A
Centre West ①
+31 (0)10 213 50 44
thetealab.nl

Don't be fooled by the name. In addition to a nice tea selection, this restaurant also serves an excellent lunch. With big sandwiches and healthy salad bowls. Gluten-free and vegan options available.

The 5 favourite places of
VEGETARIANS

---

11 **SPIRIT**
AT: DE GROENE PASSAGE
Mariniersweg 9
Centre East ②
+31 (0)10 411 63 56
spiritrotterdam.nl

This upscale canteen is located in the Groene Passage (a sustainable shopping centre) and serves 100% vegetarian and organic food. The concept is quite simple: saunter past the buffet and take your pick of over 50 fresh dishes, hot and cold, sweet and savoury. Let your eyes and nose decide and pay by the weight you put on your plate.

12 **GARE DU NORD**
Anthoniestraat 2
North ③
+31 (0)10 310 62 88
restaurant
garedunord.nl

No meat, no fish, no dairy: Gare du Nord serves a purely vegan three course menu that changes daily. Part of its appeal is its setting in an old German train wagon in an urban oasis that includes a vegetable patch and a nice terrace.

13 **VEGGIE**
Frits Ruysstraat 16-A
Northeast ④
+31 (0)6 411 244 96
veggierotterdam.com

This vegan and Brazilian-inspired coffee and lunch place was an instant neighbourhood favourite. Owner Monica hails from Brazil and is a true animal lover, that's why she serves cruelty-free fare with Latin American flair. Part of the profits and all tips go to an animal rescue charity.

14 RESTAURANT ROTONDE

Goudsesingel 230
Centre East ②
+31 (0)6 493 972 69
restaurantrotonde.nl

Locally sourced vegetables, grains and pulses served in the purest possible way, accompanied by a glass of natural wine. The veggies really take centre stage in this shared-dining concept. Rotonde is probably one of the most exciting and experimental veggie restaurants in town.

15 DE KADE

West-Kruiskade 17-B
Centre West ①
+31 (0)10 845 32 39
dekaderotterdam.nl

Restaurant De Kade has a fresh look and serves vegetarian fare inspired by Chinese, Vietnamese and Surinamese cuisine. The menu goes on for several pages and the dishes are simply mouth-watering. Stop here for a quick Surinamese sandwich, a soup or an Asian snack, or tuck into a healthy vegetarian meal with mushrooms or faux meat.

12 GARE DU NORD

The 5 best places to eat
FRESH FISH

---

16   **A LA PLANCHA**
Van der Takstraat 2
South ⑤
+31 (0)6 412 655 09
alaplancha.nl

This laidback fish and tapas restaurant on Noordereiland started as an outdoor neighbourhood initiative near Willems Bridge. Since 2022 it has settled down in an attractive corner building. Neighbours and regulars are shareholders, and food is locally sourced, where possible.

17   **BRASSERIE KAAT MOSSEL**
Admiraliteitskade 85
Northeast ④
+31 (0)10 404 86 00
kaatmossel.nl

Nothing seems to have changed for decades in this cosy, living room-like restaurant with a view of the yacht harbour. This brasserie is famous for its mussels, and there are many options to choose from: mussels in white wine, baked mussels with curry masala or stir fried mussels. The menu also includes meat, fish and vegetarian dishes.

18 PACIFIC FISH

1e Middelland-
straat 118
West ⑥
+31 (0)10 737 05 79
pacificfish.nl

A tastefully decorated fishmonger, restaurant and caterer in one. Famed for its *kibbeling* (fried cod bites) and its homemade paella (among others), Pacific Fish is definitely one of those little gems on Middellandstraat. Enjoy one of the many freshly prepared fish dishes in the blue-tiled interior.

19 KAAP

Delistraat 48
South ⑤
+31 (0)10 423 22 22
localekaap.nl

The concrete walls and simple furniture of this 'fish hall' make for a basic setting. The presentation may be no frills but the fish steaks, fruits de mer, lobsters, oysters or fish soup are all of superb quality. Order a side of fries, pick a wine from their nice selection and you're good to go. The menu also has some vegetarian options.

20 ZEEZOUT

Westerkade 11
Centre West ①
+31 (0)10 436 50 49
restaurantzeezout.nl

This restaurant in a stately corner building with a view of the River Maas serves exquisite fish and shellfish dishes with a Rotterdam twist, using local ingredients. Owner and chef Patrick 't Hart has worked hard to turn this place into the best fish restaurant of Rotterdam. The dishes and the presentation are mouth-watering.

5 great restaurants with a
MODERN CUISINE

21 **PUTAINE**
AT: FLOATING OFFICE
ROTTERDAM
Antoine
Platekade 996
South ⑤
+31 (0)6 285 105 45
restaurantputaine.nl

Putaine has its own swimming pool, but that's certainly not the only draw. It has been wowing customers with its delicate cuisine, serving small and seasonal dishes since its opening in 2021. As it is located in the Floating Office in Rijnhaven, stunning views are guaranteed.

22 **RESTAURANT RENILDE**
AT: DEPOT BOIJMANS
VAN BEUNINGEN
Museumpark 24
Centre West ①
boijmans.nl/depot/
restaurant

Chef Jim de Jong (formerly of restaurant De Jong) cooks a 4-, 5-, or 6-course menu for his guests on top of Museum Boijmans Van Beuningen's shining storage depot, shaped like a huge salad bowl. The view is exceptional, and the quality of the food is consistently high. Vegetarian options available.

23 EAUX POSSE

Schiemond 40-B
West ⑥
+31 (0)10 737 18 15
eauxposse.nl

In their own words, Eaux Posse serves food that is 'simple yet complex, casual yet refined, artisanal yet modern'. Perhaps more importantly, the French and Spanish-inspired dishes taste great, the ambiance is amazing and the location is off the beaten track, with a great view of the harbour.

24 MEVROUW MEIJER

Gerard Scholten-
straat 37-B
North ③
+31 (0)10 466 33 67
mevrouwmeijer.nl

The white curtains and little tables give this intimate restaurant a French vibe. What's more, the menu is actually very French, with a modern twist. You might find homemade blood sausage on the menu or oysters and langoustines, fresh out of the sea. There's a nice selection of wines by the glass.

25 LUX

's-Gravendijkwal 133
West ⑥
+31 (0)10 476 22 06
restaurantlux.nl

Chef Milan Gataric was inspired by the gastronomical traditions of Rome's slaughterhouse neighbourhood, Testaccio. He uses basic ingredients and traditional methods like salt aging and artisan fermenting. The menu also includes *offal*. The spaghetti with grated tuna heart is a speciality of the house, but there are less adventurous options like home-cured meats and fresh fish as well.

5 of the most sophisticated
FINE DINING
restaurants

---

26 RESTAURANT FRED
Honingerdijk 263
Northeast ④
+31 (0)10 212 01 10
restaurantfred.nl

Step into this Michelin**-starred restaurant with its world class gastronomy, modern, baroque-styled interior and skilled service. Chef Fred Mustert was inspired by traditional French gastronomy, but added a personal twist.

27 PARKHEUVEL
Heuvellaan 21
Centre West ①
+31 (0)10 436 07 66
parkheuvel.nl

Parkheuvel combines a great location, on the corner of the elegant park near the Euromast, with culinary experience. The restaurant, run by chef Erik van Loo, has two Michelin stars and has been a byword for fine dining since 1990.

28 FOOD LABS BY FRANÇOIS GEURDS
Katshoek 41
North ③
+31 (0)10 425 05 20
fgfoodlabs.nl

François Geurds is one of the top chefs that has given Rotterdam's haute cuisine a new impulse. Rewarded many times over (Food Labs currently has one Michelin star), Geurds is always trying to come up with innovative taste experiences and has his own taste laboratory on site. Food Labs offers lunch as well as dinner menus, with vegetarian options available.

29 JOELIA
AT: HILTON ROTTERDAM
Coolsingel 5
Centre West ①
+31 (0)10 710 80 34
joelia.eu

This lavishly decorated restaurant by chef Mario Ridder is located on the ground floor of the Hilton Hotel. It has a fantastic wine selection and was awarded a Michelin star. The modern French-style menu includes Wagyu meat, North Sea sole and other ingredients that Ridder has been using for years, as well as new and innovative dishes that change with the seasons.

30 FITZGERALD
Gelderseplein 49
Centre East ②
+31 (0)10 268 70 10
restaurant
fitzgerald.com

Named after the famous author F. Scott Fitzgerald who appreciated a good drink, this restaurant has been racking up awards since its opening in 2015. It holds a Michelin star and its wine selection has received many accolades. The interior is retro chic, the dishes modern and exciting, using bold combinations.

The 5 best places to enjoy
LATIN AMERICAN FOOD

31 **SABOR SABOR**
Adrien Milder-
straat 11-A
West ⑥
+31 (0)6 156 200 25
saborsabor.nl

Enjoy authentic Mexican cuisine in this cosy family restaurant located in a quiet square in Rotterdam West. Chef Liz Derflingher opened Sabor Sabor after moving to The Netherlands from Mexico City. Expect freshly baked corn tortillas, exquisite Margaritas, and dishes with crickets.

33 LA BANDERA

32 BOTANERO

Mariniersweg 55
Centre East ②
+31 (0)10 720 09 20
botanerorotterdam.com

Enjoy delicious cocktails at Botanero – from classics like a Margarita or Pornstar Martini, to the self-invented Paloma made with tequila, grapefruit soda, lime and salt. For those who prefer their liquor neat there is a wide selection of artisanal mezcals and tequilas. Order some of their delicious tacos or small snacks *(botanas)* to share.

33 LA BANDERA

Nieuwe Binnen-
weg 285-A
West ⑥
+31 (0)10 795 51 11
labandera.nl

Fried chicken with *cassave* and *tostones*, homemade lemonade, fried banana with caramel for dessert and Dominican black coffee with a pinch of cinnamon to top of your meal. In La Bandera you get the full Dominican experience in a relaxed and friendly setting.

34 ALFREDO'S TAQUERIA

Goudsesingel 204
Centre East ②
+31 (0)10 307 46 80
alfredostaqueria.nl

Alfredo's Taqueria has an extensive menu that includes tasty tacos like the Al Pastor, filled with spicy pork belly (or a vegan alternative) and the Hongos with marinated mushrooms. The cocktail bar serves a variety of tequilas and mezcals, as well as Margaritas and a *carajillo* cocktail with espresso. Make sure to check out their cosy terrace when the weather is nice.

35 JUST

Mauritsweg 53-B
Centre West ①
+31 (0)6 402 644 97
justrotterdam.nl

Hailing from Curaçao, Chef Justin had already become somewhat of a TV celebrity (by competing in the Dutch MasterChef) before starting his own Caribbean soul food restaurant in Rotterdam. A local newspaper deemed this place 'close to comfort food heaven'. Open till late on weekends.

5 places to eat
AROUND THE WORLD

---

36 **HELAI**
    Piet Smitkade 160
    South ⑤
    +31 (0)10 482 34 66
    helai.nl

Located deep in Rotterdam South, near the Van Brienenoord bridge, you'll find this hidden gem of an Afghan restaurant. Enjoy the fabulous 1001-night-themed decor while you fill up on traditional Afghan dishes. The menu is quite heavy on the meat dishes, but there are some veggie options available as well.

37 **INJERA HABESHA**
    Hudsonplein 7-B
    West ⑥
    +31 (0)6 876 805 65
    injerahabesha.com

Injera is the name of the pillar of Ethiopian cuisine: a very thin pancake made of *teff* (a type of grain). Habesha serves a variety of dishes that you eat by using your hands to scoop them up with bits of the pancake, which serves as your plate. Don't forget to sample some traditional Ethiopian coffee as well.

38 URUMQI

Diergaardesingel 93-B
Centre West ①
+31 (0)10 210 97 90
urumqirestaurant.nl

Named after the capital of Xinjiang, Urumqi is the first Uyghur restaurant in The Netherlands. The cuisine is a mixture of West and East Asia: think rice dishes with chicken or lamb, but also a hearty beef and onion pie or stir-fries with homemade noodles.

39 BALKAN DELI

Westzeedijk 381-J
West ⑥
+31 (0)6 147 004 69
balkandeli.nl

Whether you're feeling homesick, nostalgic about your last holiday in one of the Balkan countries, or just eager to try something new: Balkan Deli offers hearty and homemade fare, like bread with *cevapcici* sausages, goulash and *sopska* salad. They also have a good wine selection.

40 CAFÉ MARSEILLE

1e Middelland-
straat 16-B
Centre West ①
+31 (0)10 841 30 81
cafemarseille.nl

A culinary trip around the world isn't complete without French cuisine. At Marseille, they've distilled it to its purest form, serving classic fare like *poulet rôti* (roast chicken), fish soup and lobster and, on Sundays, cheap oysters. A big plus is the sizeable terrace that is perfect for people-watching.

The 5 best places to sample
ASIAN CUISINE

───────

41 **YAMA**
Eendrachtsweg 31-A
Centre West ①
+31 (0)6 213 724 51
jcyama.com

Japanese haute cuisine, served in an intimate setting where you can watch the chef at work. Diners sit at the long bar and eat a seven-course set menu that can be paired with sake. This restaurant pays the utmost attention to quality, taste, presentation and service and is very popular. Reserve a month in advance.

42 **TENSAI RAMEN**
Schiedamsedijk 1
Centre West ①
+31 (0)10 844 91 40

It's a hotly debated topic among *ramen* lovers: where can you score the best bowl of Japanese noodle soup? Our favourite is Tensai Ramen. Their secret? The noodles are made on the spot, using an imported machine, and each *ramen* dish has its own type of noodle. Their broth is also delicious, subtle and not too salty.

43 **BAP BOSS**
Goudsesingel 26
Centre East ②
+31 (0)10 316 05 49
bapboss.nl

While a lot of Korean restaurants in The Netherlands focus solely on grilled meat, Bap Boss also caters to seafood and tofu lovers with an extensive menu – although their meat is excellent, too. Try the seafood pancake or the spicy tofu stew, for example.

44 PHO HANOI

Botersloot 58-A
Centre East ②
+31 (0)10 846 93 08
phohanoi.nl

Chef Minh Le serves dishes from North-Vietnamese cuisine, like *bánh mì* (Vietnamese sandwiches), bun noodles and variations on the national dish *pho*: a noodle soup filled with beef, chicken or meat balls. A hearty, nutritious and spicy dish that's a good antidote for an oncoming flu or head cold. Try one of the fresh spring rolls as well.

45 KAMPONG EXPRESS

Gouvernestraat 2-B
Centre West ①
+31 (0)10 752 39 78
kampongexpress.nl

This charming little eatery specialises in *nasi lemak* (rice boiled in coconut milk, served in a *pandan* leaf), which is a Malaysian breakfast dish, but can be eaten any time of day. The same goes for *jian bing,* Chinese savoury pancakes served by Super Crepe, now part of the same restaurant.

The 5 best
CHINESE
restaurants

46 **SĀNSĀN**
Hang 33
Centre East ②
+31 (0)10 411 56 81
sansan33.nl

Don't be shocked by the fish heads, jellyfish or duck's tongues on the menu; some food critics consider sānsān to be one of the best Chinese restaurants in the country. The chefs cook according to traditional recipes from the Sichuan region in southern China, a cuisine with spicy dishes.

47 **TAI WU**
Mauritsweg 24-26
Centre West ①
+31 (0)10 433 08 18
tai-wu.nl

This huge restaurant covers two floors and looks like any other kitsch Dutch-Chinese restaurant, including Buddha statues and an aquarium filled with carps. But don't be fooled, the menu features a wealth of tasty dishes, including dim sum, Peking duck and seafood. The steamed oysters with garlic or black beans are a favourite.

48 ASIAN GLORIES

Leeuwenstraat 15
Centre East ②
+31 (0)10 411 71 07
asianglories.nl

Asian Glories serves elegant dinners in a modern, Chinese setting. Through the open kitchen, you can see the chefs prepare your steamed razor clams, oysters, or scallops with noodles. There's also a nice selection of handmade dim sum and vegetarian food to choose from.

49 MY FONG TOKO

West-Kruiskade 52
Centre West ①
+31 (0)10 241 74 88
myfongtoko.nl

This low-key caterer in the centre of the Chinese district is very popular with the Chinese community and can get very crowded. Peking duck, roasted pork, sticky rice with chicken rolled in a green leaf and other homemade dishes are boxed and displayed in the counter. Most people order take-away, but there are also some tables inside.

50 LITTLE ASIA

Kleiweg 87-A
North ③
+31 (0)10 422 62 63
lilasia.nl

The spicy Singapore crab and Peking duck are just two of the specialties of this Cantonese restaurant in Hillegersberg, but there's a wealth of dim sum and pork dishes to choose from as well. The restaurant is small, so book in advance or order a take-out.

The 5 best places for great
FRENCH FRIES

51 **SCHIPPER PATAT**
Karel Doormanstraat /
Korte Lijnbaan
Centre West ①
+31 (0)6 517 850 23

Frans Schipper has been baking fries since 1979 and has perfected the art. His fries, crispy on the outside and soft and tasty on the inside, are a real treat and a very good reason not to hurry past windy and slippery Schouwburgplein.

52 **BRAM LADAGE**
KOP VAN ZUID
Posthumalaan 90
South ⑤
+31 (0)6 262 950 78
bramladage.nl

Bram Ladage's hand-cut fresh fries were already famous, when in 2016 the Ladages set themselves a new challenge: gourmet fries. In a sea container on the river's south bank you can order fries with Asian chicken stew, pulled pork, or a veggie stew with mushrooms. The freshly made crispy golden fries still steal the show.

53 **FRIETBOUTIQUE**
Witte de With-
straat 68-A
Centre West ①
+31 (0)10 310 62 58
frietboutique.nl

If you could only eat deep-fried snacks every day, make them Frietboutique snacks. The fries are thick and crispy, and their snacks, especially their aged cheese croquette or *frikandel speciaal* (also available in vegan option) are to die for. Do try the amazing truffle mayonnaise with your fries.

54 POMMS'

Coolsingel 107-B
Centre West ①
+31 (0)6 286 66 29
pomms.nl

The tastiest organic fries and croquettes in the country! At least, that's the status Pomms' aspires to. Go and judge for yourself and order a *puntzak friet,* a portion of freshly cut fries baked with the skin on. The croquettes come in different flavours including beef, shrimp and goat's cheese. They're completely organic and devoid of additives.

55 TANTE NEL

Pannekoekstraat 53
Centre East ②
+31 (0)10 846 02 65
tante-nel-rotterdam.nl

This is the perfect spot for a snack after a day of shopping in the Blaak area. They serve fresh fries, croquettes (also veggie), a *patat stoofvlees* (fries with meat stew) and even fries with caviar! As a finishing touch, you can order alcoholic beverages and cocktails. Or a milkshake with rum.

52 BRAM LADAGE KOP VAN ZUID

The 5 nicest places to go for a
QUICK BITE

---

56 LA CABANE DE FABIAN

Bergweg 152-A
North ③
+31 (0)10 223 76 73
lacabanedefabian
rotterdam.nl

A deli, breakfast bar and sandwich shop all rolled into one. Fabian serves crispy fresh bread generously topped with Mediterranean style meats, cheese and fresh veg in surprising and tasty combinations. You can get a sandwich and a few delicacies to go, or sit down at one of the tables upstairs.

57 FILO-FILO

Nieuwe Binnen-
weg 230-A
West ⑥
+31 (0)10 786 57 94
filo-filo.nl

This small eatery specialises in *bougatsa*, a Greek delicacy. Layers of fluffy puff pastry are filled with feta cheese, spinach, minced meat or sausage. If you have a sweet tooth, try the *bougatsa* with custard or with chocolate and hazelnut. In summer, have a very good *freddo* (iced espresso) with your *bougatsa* in the back garden.

58 LITTLE ITALY

Lombardkade 51-A
Centre East ②
+31 (0)10 413 96 09

You have to know it to spot it, since Little Italy is situated just a little off the Meent. But once you've set foot inside this Italian deli you'll keep on coming back for more. The Italian meats, cheeses, pasta and wines are excellent. As are the sandwiches that always draw a lunchtime crowd.

59 BOGUETTE

Botersloot 60-A
Centre East ②
+31 (0)10 841 79 10
boguette.nl

This tiny sandwich shop combines the best of two worlds: French baguettes and Vietnamese street food. Boguette serves tasteful *bánh mì* (Vietnamese sandwiches), filled with spicy meat or tofu, fresh herbs and vegetables. Looking for something lighter? Try a salad or roll. Boguette also serves several bubble teas, the Taiwanese hot or cold tea with milk or fruit juice.

60 PISTACHE HALAB

Nieuwe Binnen-
weg 289-A
West ⑥
+31 (0)10 210 45 40
pistachehalab.nl

It's hard to choose a favourite among all the good Syrian places that have opened up in Rotterdam over the past few years, but Pistache Halab is currently at the top of our list. A family-friendly restaurant with outstanding shoarma, very good falafel and numerous side dishes.

The 5 best places to enjoy
SURINAMESE FOOD

---

61 **ASHA**
    Bergweg 357
    North ③
    +31 (0)10 465 52 31
    asha-afhaal.nl

Rotterdam has a large Surinamese community and lots of places to go for Surinamese food. Asha is popular for its freshly made and well filled *bara*, a dough snack made of peas and spices. Other traditional dishes on the menu include *roti* (pancakes with potatoes, vegetables and meat), *moksi meti* (mixed meat) and some good vegetarian dishes.

62 **ROTILAND**
    Gerrit Jan Mulder-straat 2-A
    West ⑥
    +31 (0)10 477 82 11
    rotiland-rotterdam.nl

Don't be overwhelmed by the astounding number of different roti dishes on the menu here, just keep coming back to try them all. Vegetarians also have ample choice, but we do suggest trying the roti roll with veggies, tempeh and pumpkin first. Order to take away.

63 WARUNG MINI

**Witte de With-
straat 47
Centre West ①
+31 (0)10 413 28 86
*warungmini.com***

This Surinamese-Indonesian restaurant has been serving a wide variety of customers – from men in business suits and Surinamese families to students – since the 1980s. It's a popular spot that can get crowded. Just walk up to the counter, place an order, find a seat and wait for your bowl of *saoto* chicken soup, *roti*, or a baked banana with homemade peanut sauce.

64 WARUNG GARENG

**Schiedamseweg 40-A
West ⑥
+31 (0)10 818 37 21
*warunggareng.nl***

Their *saoto* soup with chicken and rice is unrivalled, and is the perfect remedy for when you're feeling a bit under the weather. Try a *roti* if you're hungry and don't forget to order a baked banana with homemade peanut sauce on the side. You'll probably leave feeling a bit stuffed, but oh so happy.

65 WONG'S PLACE

**Jonker Frans-
straat 82-A
North ③
+31 (0)10 214 28 53**

This Chinese-Surinamese eating house is run by friendly Ramon Wong, who moved to the Netherlands in the 1980s. It's been a popular spot for quite some time. The menu includes Surinamese classics like *pom* (salted meat and tayer root), *telo* (dried and salted fish) and the often praised chicken curry on a sandwich or with *roti*.

The 5 best places for a
DELICIOUS PIZZA

66 **LA PIZZA**
Scheepstimmermans-
laan 21
Centre West ①
+31 (0)10 241 77 97
lapizza.nl

This restaurant has a no-nonsense interior design, pleasant service, and a classy restaurant vibe that is sometimes lacking in your local pizzeria. The pizzas have crispy crusts and come in small or large. The menu also contains a variety of other Italian dishes and a good selection of wines.

67 **ANGELO BETTI**
Schiekade 6-B
North ③
+31 (0)10 465 81 74
angelobetti.nl

Angelo Betti has been a household name since 1922 (!). People flock here from far and wide and don't mind waiting for a table. This family restaurant serves crispy pizzas with generous toppings (heavy on the cheese) and is famed for its homemade ice cream. Expect to leave this place feeling very contented and stuffed.

68 O'PAZZO

Mariniersweg 90
Centre East ②
+31 (0)10 282 71 07
opazzo.nl

These real Napolitan pizzas are rolled out on marble slabs and baked in an octopus-shaped wood oven. The pizzas are like pizzas are supposed to be, with soft upstanding edges, a crispy tasty base and stringy cheese that is just right. Pizzas are served both for lunch and dinner.

69 DE BUFFEL

Middellandplein 19-A
West ⑥
+31 (0)10 750 06 28
debuffelrotterdam.nl

De Buffel serves wood-fired pizzas that are close to perfection. Try the La Norma (with aubergine) or the Porcini Tartufo (mushrooms and truffle) if you want something other than classic pizza toppings. Their octopus starter is already quite famous, as is the excellent tiramisu, to top off your meal.

70 LA GAETANO

Prins Hendrik-
kade 113-B
South ⑤
+31 (0)10 213 53 08
lagaetano.nl

A warm and friendly family restaurant with excellent service located on Noorder-eiland. Locals don't like to share this secret and we can see why. The pizzas are tasty and affordable, and you can enjoy a full meal for less than 20 euro.

The 5 best places for a
TASTY BURGER

---

71 TER MARSCH & CO
Witte de With-straat 70
Centre West ①
termarschco.nl

Ter Marsch & Co has probably won more awards (best burger, best fries) than there are burgers on the menu. The burgers and steaks might be slightly more expensive than at your regular burger place, but they are of superior quality. Take the 'Burgeresse' burger, which includes Scottish angus beef, Japanese Wagyu and pancetta. All burgers can be ordered with a veggie alternative.

72 BURGERTRUT
Delftseplein 39
Centre West ①
roodkapje.org/burgertrut

This slightly artsy, easy-going and affordable burger joint was started by the adjacent Roodkapje art and music venue, so your cash will support the arts. The menu includes organic, vegetarian and vegan burgers, and even veggie or vegan *kapsalon* (a local treat, made of French fries topped with shoarma meat and melted cheese).

73 HAMBURG

Witte de With-straat 94-B
Centre West ①
+31 (0)10 737 15 37
restauranthamburg.nl

They were among the first restaurants of the recent hamburger wave that swept Rotterdam (in particular the Witte de With area), and Hamburg hasn't changed much since opening in 2014. The ingredients are fresh and of high quality, the setting is basic. The menu also includes vegetarian options.

74 DIEGO'S

Posthumalaan 3
South ⑤
+31 (0)10 254 00 74
diegosburgers.com

Diego Buik, the man behind this burger joint at Kop van Zuid, has won several prizes. The most remarkable is the award for most expensive burger in the world: his white truffle, caviar, lobster, foie gras and gold leaf burger costs 2050 euro. Luckily, Diego's tricks in Rotterdam are more affordable and just as tasty.

75 BURGER CLUB

Nieuwe Binnen-weg 139-A
Centre West ①
+31 (0)10 841 15 82
burgerclub.nl

A specific Dutch cattle breed, Japanese Wagyu beef or Iberico pork: at Burger Club you can select the meat you like best. The taste of the meat is what makes these luxurious burgers so special. The sauces only enhance it. The menu also includes fresh French fries, a vegetarian weed burger and a fine selection of gin and tonics.

5
LOCAL SPECIALITIES
you should try

---

76 **APPLE PIE**
AT: DUDOK
Meent 88
Centre East ②
+31 (0)10 433 31 02
dudok.nl

Dudok's famous apple pie is made with natural ingredients and has a tasty, crumbling crust. The cream that comes with it is freshly made. This grand cafe's name refers to the architect Willem Dudok, who designed this iconic, post-war building with its characteristic high ceilings and windows.

77 **UIERBOORD**
AT: SALGERIJ OOTEMAN
Oude Binnen-
weg 123-A
Centre West ①
+31 (0)10 414 79 43
slagerij-ooteman.nl

Uierboord is made of a cow's udder, which is boiled for 12 hours and then roasted. It's difficult to find this Rotterdam treat nowadays, but butcher Ooteman still serves it. Order uierboord on a bun, with some salt and pepper.

78 KAPSALON
AT: EL AVIVA
Schiedamseweg 22-A
West ⑥
+31 (0)10 425 89 05
elaviva-rotterdam.nl

At the beginning of this century, a hairdresser in Schiedamseweg was hungry but couldn't decide what he wanted. He then called his neighbours at snack bar El Aviva, and asked for a mix of everything: shawarma, cheese, garlic and fries. The result, *kapsalon* (Dutch for hairdresser's), became a Rotterdam treat and a national hype.

79 MAASSTROOMPJES
+31 (0)6 177 318 88
maasstroompjes.nl

The official Rotterdam cookie since 1934 was originally sold by pastry baker G. Slob on the Nieuwe Binnenweg. In 2013, his granddaughter, Inge Bodmer, decided to give the slightly forgotten cookie a new lease on life. The new Maasstroompjes are 100% organic, as close to the original as possible and sold in attractively designed boxes. Check the website for points of sale.

80 JENEVER
TRY: HENKES

Schiedam was the centre of Dutch *jenever* production for centuries. But Rotterdam also had its own distilleries such as Henkes, that used to be located in Delfshaven. Henkes Jenever is now part of the large Bols distillery family and bottles of Henkes are available in most liquor stores.

5 of the most fabulous
BAKERIES and
PASTRY SHOPS

---

81 JORDY'S BAKERY
**Nieuwe Binnen-
weg 97-A**
Centre West ⓘ
+31 (0)10 225 09 52
jordysbakery.nl

Jordy Klootwijk was born into a baker's family. In 2011, he opened his own bakery and lunchroom. People queue here to buy sourdough bread, but you can also sit down and enjoy a toasted sourdough sandwich. Finish your meal with a macadamia cookie or a brownie.

82 DAS BROT
Gouvernestraat 246
Centre West ⓘ
dasbrot.nl

Sourdough, sourdough and more sourdough. At Das Brot they make artisan breads with a long rise time. The excellent croissants and *pains au chocolat* also may take up to three days to reach perfection. Das Brot has a steadily growing fan base.

83 KOEKELA

Nieuwe Binnen-
weg 79-A
Centre West ①
+31 (0)10 436 47 74
koekela.nl

Californian native Sereni Horton moved to Rotterdam for love and started her own pastry shop where she combines American staples like cookies, brownies, blondies, and lemon bars with a Rotterdam no nonsense attitude. People who've tasted her magic cookie bar, made of pure and white chocolate, cranberries, raisins and pecan nuts keep coming back for more.

84 LOF DER ZOETHEID

Noordplein 1
North ③
+31 (0)6 232 901 80
lofderzoetheid.com

Mother-and-daughter team Elena and Anastasia de Ruyter only bake and serve what they like, because life's too short to eat bad food. They use local and organic produce. They serve breakfast and lunch, but are most famous for their afternoon tea with breads, cakes, chocolates, scones, quiche and a Russian *samovar*. Reserve ahead.

85 AAP NOOT BROOD

Schiemond 42-A
West ⑥
aapnootbrood.nl

Locals get their fresh and organic sourdough bread through a subscription, while passers-by settle down for a cup of coffee and excellent pastries. Big plusses are the bright blue interior and a terrace overlooking the River Maas. Open Wednesday through Saturday.

The 5 cosiest
FOOD MARKETS

---

86 AFRIKAANDERPLEIN MARKET
Afrikaanderplein
South ⑤

All the world lives in Rotterdam, and the south bank without a doubt is the city's most diverse neighbourhood. The market in Afrikaanderplein, on Wednesdays and Saturdays, is a hotchpotch of the city's diverse communities and their culinary traditions.

87 ROTTERDAMSE OOGSTMARKT
Noordplein
North ③
+31 (0)10 841 89 08
rotterdamseoogst.nl

Fresh bread, meat and vegetables: these and many other regionally grown or produced products are sold at this farmer's market. You can sample anything from wild goose sausages to soy saté and fresh oysters. It's held every Saturday at Noordplein.

88 KAAPSE MARKT
Deliplein
South ⑤

On Fridays from 10 am till 5 pm, Deliplein hosts a lively market. The municipality started this initiative in 2022 because the inhabitants of Katendrecht wanted their own food market, with wares from local producers and with more atmosphere and less waste.

89 BINNENROTTE CENTRUMMARKT
Binnenrotte
Centre East ②

Between 400 and 500 stalls are set up every Tuesday and Saturday at Binnenrotte from 8 am to 5.30 pm, next to Blaak station and Markthal, making it one of the largest outdoor markets in the country. A wealth of fresh vegetables and fruits, meat and fish, nuts, tasty snacks and whatever else you can think of is for sale here.

90 ORGANIC MARKET
Eendrachtsplein 12
Centre West ①

Every Tuesday from 8.30 am to 5.30 pm there's a small *biologische markt* (organic market) at Eendrachtsplein. On offer are breads and pastries, dairy and cheese, vegetables and fruit, and meat. The organic produce is made with respect for nature, without pesticides and fertilisers.

89 BINNENROTTE CENTRUMMARKT

The 5 most
MOUTH-WATERING
STANDS *at the* MARKTHAL

MARKTHAL
Ds. Jan Scharpstraat 298
Centre East ②
markthal.nl

91 **55 BOMBAY STREET**
Unit 55
+31 (0)6 843 506 41
55bombaystreet-
rotterdam.nl

Homemade and 100% vegetarian/vegan:
55 Bombay Street sells Indian classics
like *samosa, paani puri, palak paneer* and
various chutneys. The food is fresh, very
affordable and extremely tasty.

MARKTHAL

92 OBBA'S FOODBAR

Unit 73-75
obbasfoodbar.nl

The Obba Lounge is a hidden gem on the river's south bank (located at Hillelaan 2) that serves Mediterranean delicacies in a peculiar construction of sea containers under a nomad-like tent. Their stall at the Markthal is equally worth visiting. On the menu are plates with grilled meat, Turkish *mezze* and other tasty dishes.

93 NATAMANIA

Unit 47
+31 (0)6 455 420 73
natamania.nl

Natamania sells products from Portugal like wine, olive oil and attractively designed cans of sardines. But the *pastel de nata* is the real star of this stall: creamy, crunchy and sweet (but not too sweet, as it should be). Order a strong espresso on the side.

94 SPICES OF MARRAKECH

Unit 50
+31 (0)6 444 306 13
spicesofmarrakech.nl

The family-owned Spices of Marrakech proves that the Markthal is still the place to go for quality groceries. They sell spices from all four corners of the world: from the Middle East to Mexico, and from Thailand to South Africa. Just follow your nose to find them.

95 INFINITEA

Unit 51
+31 (0)6 392 369 55
infinitea-markthal.nl

Use your nose. It's the best way to decide which tea to buy from this tea shop that's owned by SiYun Chang and Thanh Nguyen. These young entrepreneurs have a selection of about 40 kinds of organic, loose teas, which they change every now and then. They also sell freshly made (ice) tea.

The 5 best
ICE-CREAM
shops

---

96 **VENEZIA**
Oude Binnen-
weg 125-B
Centre West ①
+31 (0)10 411 20 23
veneziaijssalon.nl

Venezia has been a true ice-cream institution since its establishment at Eendrachtsplein in 1964. Place a quick order at the counter and enjoy their artisan ice creams on the patio, or choose something from the wide selection of ice-cream cups, cakes or homemade gelato with an espresso on the side, liquor and cream *cassatas*.

97 **IJSSALON NINO**
Paul Krüger-
straat 97-A
South ⑤
+31 (0)6 339 289 95
ijssalonnino.nl

This Italian-owned ice-cream parlour has been serving homemade ice creams and excellent espressos in Afrikaanderplein in Rotterdam South for decades. The wide variety of flavours are all made without chemicals or preservatives, and includes classics such as chocolate or Malaga to changing recipes.

98 IJSSALON DOPPIO

Crooswijkseweg 100
Northeast ④
+31 (0)10 413 44 17
ijssalondoppio.nl

Doppio hasn't left Crooswijk since 1970, but is now run by a former barista. This means that you can order tasty ice creams and great coffee as well. All ice cream is homemade with cream (like chocolate or apple pie) or without cream (fruit). Doppio has a second shop at Lusthofstraat 71 in Kralingen.

99 CAPRI

Karel Doorman-
straat 334
Centre West ①
+31 (0)10 412 66 58
capri.nl

In addition to ice-cream classics like strawberry or pistachio, Carpi has its own trademarks. What to think of the mandorlato, made of honey, chocolate and home-roasted, candied nuts?
Capri has been serving homemade ice creams since 1957. It has a second shop in Middellandplein.

100 DE IJSSALON

Meent 69-A
Centre East ②
+31 (0)10 413 35 44
deijssalon.nl

On sunny days, people queue here to taste the IJssalon's famous cherry and chocolate, Oreo cookies or grandma's apple pie ice-cream flavours. Everything's homemade, with fresh milk, fruit, juices and herbs. Some of the flavours have been adapted to the neighbourhood's tastes. The location at West-Kruiskade 60 has Fernandes-ice cream on the menu, named after the popular soft drink from Surinam.

HAAL HENKES IN HUIS

CAFÉ DE OOIEVAAR

60 PLACES TO GO FOR A DRINK

———

The 5 best
COCKTAIL BARS

---

101 TIKI'S BAR

Hartmansstraat 16-A
Centre East ②
+31 (0)10 201 95 76

Tiki's has such a diverse range of customers that it's hard to predict whom you'll meet. On weekends, this bar is packed with people of all ages and backgrounds, enjoying a beer or a cocktail. The menu ranges from classic cocktails like a Mojito and a Margarita to the Godfather (Amaretto and Jack Daniels) and the Banana Daiquiri with fresh banana and rum.

102 SPIKIZI

Zwarte Paarden-
straat 91-A
Centre West ①
+31 (0)6 145 427 92
spikizibar.com

A hole-in-the-wall speakeasy, just off Witte de Withstraat, that can get a bit crowded on the weekend. Spikizi has built up quite the fan base in Rotterdam with their cocktails and mocktails. Try one with mezcal or kombucha for something different.

103 THE RUMAH

Oude Binnen-
weg 110-C
Centre West ⓘ
*therumah
rotterdam.com*

Rumah means home in Bahasa, Indonesia's language, and that's exactly the vibe this bar is going for: a homey neighbour-hood feel. This is one of those places where you could hang out all night with friends, with great cocktails to ease the conversation along.

104 OX

AT: SCHIEBLOCK
Schiekade 189
Centre West ⓘ
+31 (0)10 213 17 66
ox-rotterdam.nl

What do cocktails, dim sum and natural wines have to do with each other? Not much, at first thought, but in OX it all comes together wonderfully in a dark and stylish basement, complete with graffiti and a fish tank. Go and see it for yourself. OX can be hard to find, but you'll get instructions if you reserve ahead.

105 BALLROOM

Witte de With-
straat 88-B
Centre West ⓘ
ox-rotterdam.nl

What do cocktails, dim sum and natural wines have to do with each other? Not much, at first thought, but in OX it all comes together wonderfully in a dark and stylish basement, complete with graffiti and a fish tank. Go and see it for yourself. OX can be hard to find, but you'll get instructions if you reserve ahead.

5 places with a
GREAT BEER
SELECTION

———

106 PROEFLOKAAL FAAS
Zwaanshals 248-A
North ③
+31 (0)10 465 4711

The nicest living room bar of Rotterdam North has over a hundred bottled beers and nine draught beers. This old-fashioned pub was given a make-over and is now a nice mix of old and new, of seasoned regulars and youngsters. In the weekends there's often a DJ or band playing.

107 LOCUS PUBLICUS
Oostzeedijk 364
Northeast ④
+31 (0)10 433 17 61
locus-publicus.com

Wherever you look in this very dark traditional pub, you'll find beer bottles. The high ceiling, the dark wood interior and the fireplace make for a cosy atmosphere, especially when it's cold outside. On the menu are about 200 bottled beers and there's a changing selection of 15 draught beers.

108 BELGISCH BIERCAFÉ BOUDEWIJN
Nieuwe Binnen-weg 53-A/B
Centre West ①
+31 (0)10 436 35 62
bbcboudewijn.nl

A little piece of Belgium in Nieuwe Binnenweg: Café Boudewijn serves over 100 bottled beers and 8 draught beers, primarily from Belgium. The same goes for the menu which features Belgian specialties like shrimp croquettes, mussels and beef stew. Behind the cafe is a garden with a patio.

109 BREWPUB REIJNGOUD

Vijverhofstraat 10
North ③
+31 (0)10 503 63 27
brewpubreijngoud.nl

Proeflokaal Reijngoud at Schiedamse Vest is one of Rotterdam's most popular beer cafes and opened this second brewpub at Hofbogen. True beer aficionados will prefer this location in the northern part of town where you'll be spoiled for choice. The menu offers 40 beers on tap, over 200 in bottles, as well as pizzas and other snacks.

110 CAFÉ WALENBURG

Walenburgerweg 62-B
North ③
+31 (0)10 466 95 77
cafewalenburg
rotterdam.nl

Owner Vincent Bek single-handedly turned this cosy corner bar into a beer lover's dream. Walenburg has some 20 beers on tap, with many more bottled beers available, and is an Orval (Belgian Trappist) ambassador. According to Vincent a bar is 'Facebook 0.0': it's all about having good conversations and meeting new friends.

106 **PROEFLOKAAL FAAS**

The 5 most charming
ESPRESSO BARS

---

111 KOPI SOESOE
Sumatraweg 15
South ⑤
+31 (0)6 470 061 59
kopisoesoe.com

This cosy coffee bar annex cafe in bustling Deliplein in Katendrecht feels like your own living room. Have a strong espresso, or a *kopi soesoe*: coffee with cardamom and sweet condensed milk. Besides serving excellent coffee, Kopi Soesoe also serves Indonesian dinner on Sundays, and hosts regular events on Friday and Saturday nights.

112 COPPI
Bergweg 316
North ③
+31 (0)10 737 17 89
coppikoffie.nl

Not only is Coppi the place to go for a serious espresso or a frothy cappuccino, it's also a place where you can get your flat tyre fixed. You'll also find an answer to your more serious cycling questions and wishes, as well as a lot of creativity: Coppi sells home-designed cycling gear and coffee mugs, and occasionally organises cycling tours.

113 MR. BEANS

1e Middelland-
straat 14
Centre West ①
+31 (0)10 840 65 71
mr-beans.nl

Dutch-Moroccan comedy trio BorrelnootjeZ decided there was more to life than making YouTube sketches that have a million views and sold-out theatre shows. Like serving coffee to needy caffeine fiends, for example. They founded Mr. Beans, an oasis of cosiness near the always lively West-Kruiskade.

114 HARVEST COFFEE BREWERS

Glashaven 107
Centre East ②
harvestcoffeebrewers.nl

Whether you're looking for an exquisite cup of joe, an all-day-breakfast, or a waterfront patio: Harvest Coffee has it all. Inspired by Melbourne's coffee culture ("we obviously take our coffee seriously") and charmingly located at Leuvehaven, one of Rotterdam's many inner-city harbours.

115 URBAN ESPRESSOBAR

Nieuwe Binnen-
weg 263
West ⑥
+31 (0)6 228 145 05
urbanespressobar.nl

When Jo McCambridge moved from Australia to Rotterdam in the 90s, flat whites (that Australian speciality) or espresso bars didn't exist here yet. She decided to establish The Urban Espressobar, without any experience in the catering industry. That turned out not to be a problem: her bar is now an indispensable part of the Nieuwe Binnenweg area.

The 5 best local
COFFEE ROASTERS

---

116 MAN MET BRIL KOFFIE
Vijverhofstraat 70
North ③
manmetbrilkoffie.nl

There is always something going on at this warehouse-like coffee walhalla. In the back are large roasters filled with top quality coffee beans. Roasting usually takes place on Monday or Tuesday. You can take this coffee home with you, or just try one of their award-winning coffees while you're there.

117 HOPPER COFFEE
Zwaanshals 474
North ③
+31 (0)10 223 09 93
hopper-coffee.nl

Hopper's first location at Schiedamse Vest 146 quickly became a byword for quality coffee, homemade bread, pastries and even homemade tomato ketchup. The roasting takes place several times a month at the second location in Zwaanshals.

118 ALOHA
AT: BLUECITY
Maasboulevard 102
Centre East ②
+31 (0)10 210 81 70
alohabar.nl

The tropical atmosphere of this former swimming pool still lingers in the building and on the beautiful terrace with views of the river and bridges over the Nieuwe Maas. Aloha roasts its own coffee and often changes its bean selection. Aloha is also a bar, restaurant and patio on the river.

119 HEILIGE BOONTJES

Eendrachtsplein 3
Centre West ①
+31 (0)10 840 13 83
heiligeboontjes.com

Local socially deprived youths receive a 50-week-long training in the art of coffee by experienced baristas and roasters at this coffee bar / social project started by 'a cop and a former crook'. For these youngsters, coffee is a way to gain work experience and find more opportunities on the job market. The 'grand cafe' is aptly located in a former police station.

120 GIRAFFE COFFEE BAR

Hoogstraat 46-A
Centre East ②
+31 (0)10 307 03 44
giraffecoffee.com

You'll find Giraffe's homemade and -roasted blends in cafes throughout the city – like the Latin America Blend, which has a slightly sweet aroma, or the spicy Pacific Blend. Giraffe has their own bar in the centre, which offers all blends (packed or in a steamy cup), as well as high-quality teas and…. bike gear.

5 of the most authentic
BROWN PUBS

121 CAFÉ DE OOIEVAAR

Havenstraat 11
West ⑥
+31 (0)10 476 91 90
cafedeooievaar.nl

It's always five o'clock at Café de Ooievaar and a good time to sit down for a beer or a *jenever*. A favourite haunt of locals and visitors alike, this is one of the cosiest and inviting brown pubs Rotterdam has. And it even comes with a nice terrace!

122 CAFÉ STOBBE

Kortekade 20
Northeast ④
+31 (0)10 452 73 05
cafestobbe.nl

Stobbe is one of those places where everyone feels welcome: from politicians to students and from hockey moms to office workers. It's an old-fashioned cafe that has stood the test of time. Its dark brown interior and the starched white shirts of the waiters have remained virtually unchanged since its opening in 1942.

123 RIJKE & DE WIT

Nieuwe Binnen-
weg 332-A
West ⑥
+31 (0)10 477 05 96
rijkeendewit.nl

The history of this classic brown pub goes back a long way. Although the interior has been updated in recent years, the old charm is still visible. The old dark-brown bar is amazing, as are the beautiful stained-glass windows. Stop here for a local Man met Bril coffee or to sample one of the many beers, accompanied by a snack. In summer, the terrace offers excellent views.

124 CAFÉ DE BEL

Gerald Scholten-straat 61-B
North ③

Café de Bel is one of those neighbourhood bars with an interior that developed through the years, a soundtrack that sounds pleasantly familiar, and a crowd of young and old visitors. There are occasional music performances.

125 CAFÉ TIMMER

Oude Binnenweg 120
Centre West ①
+31 (0)10 414 11 39
cafetimmer.nl

Large parts of Oude Binnenweg were lost in the fire as a result of the bombing in May 1940. Café Timmer – its history goes back to the 1870s – was lucky that the wind changed just in time.

121 CAFÉ DE OOIEVAAR

5 places with a
STUNNING TERRACE

---

126 **PARQIET**
AT: HET PARK
Baden Powelllaan 20
Centre West ①
+31 (0)6 510 016 06
parqiet.nl

This bright and airy cafe and restaurant is located in a monumental coach house inside The Park and has a large terrace out front. It's a lovely place to sit down for a cup of locally roasted coffee, to taste a sandwich made with Jordy's Bakery bread or to watch the sun go down with a glass of wine and a shrimp croquette in hand.

130 **BIERGARTEN**

127 OKAY

Vijf Werelddelen 71
South ⑤
+31 (0)10 290 08 78
restaurant-cafe-okay.nl

The atmosphere at oKay is often lively, with the business crowd that works at Kop van Zuid having an after-work drink and locals searching for a bite to eat. This bar and restaurant is located in the renovated 19th-century warehouse De Vijf Werelddelen ('the five continents). The patio gives out on an inner harbour where pleasure boats moor.

128 WESTER PAVILJOEN

Mathenesserlaan 157
Centre West ①
+31 (0)10 436 26 45
westerpaviljoen.nl

A classic grand cafe with a very relaxed atmosphere, a kids' play area, a reading table and a large terrace. A perfect spot for a morning cappuccino and an omelette, a healthy sandwich, or a few rounds of drinks and a savoury snack.

129 CAFÉ VAN ZANTEN

Meent 44
Centre East ②
+31 (0)10 843 50 12
cafevanzanten.com

On market days (Tuesday and Saturdays) you'll have to fight for a place on this sun-drenched terrace. Café van Zanten is a lively central spot that gets a lot of sun. Once you've secured a place, it's tempting to stay here for hours, starting with coffee and ending with a beer and *bitterballen* or flammkuchen.

130 BIERGARTEN

Schiestraat 18
Centre West ①
+31 (0)10 233 05 56
biergartenrotterdam.nl

'Give the people what they want', that's the motto of this German style biergarten, and what they want is cold beer, sunshine, freshly grilled foods and music. This is one of the biggest and liveliest terraces in Rotterdam, when weather permits.

The 5 best

BARS TO WORK

with or without coffee

---

131 FLOOR
Schouwburgplein 28
Centre West ①
+31 (0)10 404 52 88
cafefloor.nl

Order coffee or a bite to eat and log on to the free Wi-Fi network of this spacious cafe-restaurant that's part of the City Theatre. Floor also has an inner courtyard garden that is a great place to work when it's sunny.

132 LEBKOV
Stationsplein 50
Centre West ①
+31 (0)10 240 06 17
lebkov.nl

Many people bring their laptops to this coffee bar annex lunch room in the monumental Groothandelsgebouw, across the street from Central Station. So grab a coffee and something sweet, some soup or salad and find yourself a place to settle down.

133 STATIONSHUISKAMER
AT: ROTTERDAM CENTRAAL
Stationsplein 1
Centre West ①
+31 (0)6 232 303 96
stationshuiskamer.nl

You can see travellers arrive in the central hall below, while working in the StationsHuiskamer in Rotterdam's Central Station. This coffee bar is nicely decorated with old train equipment, plants and trendy furniture. And don't worry about missing your train: the timetables are on the wall. Get here from platform 1 or take the escalator to the left of the service centre.

134 **LEESZAAL ROTTERDAM WEST**

Rijnhoutplein 3
Centre West ①
*leeszaal
rotterdamwest.nl*

When the local library of Rotterdam West had to close down, a group of volunteers immediately came up with an alternative. The Leeszaal (reading room) opened in 2012 and is now a vibrant place where volunteers, neighbourhood dwellers and readers of all ages and from all backgrounds meet for a cup of coffee, to borrow books, read the papers, or attend (literary) events.

135 **BISTRO BAR BINNENROTTE**

AT: CENTRALE BIBLIOTHEEK ROTTERDAM
Hoogstraat 110
Centre East ②
+31 (0)10 281 61 00
bistrobarbinnenrotte.nl

The glass and tubes architecture of Rotterdam's library in a way resembles Centre Pompidou in Paris. The rooftop patio offers an amazing view of the city. Inside you'll find Wi-Fi, newspapers and plenty of space to sit down. Work here and enjoy the remarkable building.

131 FLOOR

The 5 most fabulous
WATERFRONT TERRACES

136 **PRACHTIG**
Willemsplein 77
Centre West ①
+31 (0)10 213 06 40
prachtigrotterdam.nl

Located right next to Erasmus Bridge, this terrace offers spectacular views of the Nieuwe Maas River and the south bank with its impressive skyscrapers. Prachtig hasn't skimped on space: there are over 200 seats divided into separate lounge, lunch and dinner areas.

137 **RDM KANTINE**
Heijplaatstraat 3
South ⑤
+31 (0)10 429 18 34
rdmkantine.nl

Admire the port of Rotterdam from this waterfront terrace in the former dry docks. It's located close to where the Waterbus arrives and departs (stop: Heijplaat). RDM Kantine serves a healthy lunch, pastries and croquettes by Dudok, and has a simple drinks menu. Come on time, as they're only open during the day. Closed on weekends.

138 OUDE HAVEN

Spaansekade
Centre East ②

There are so many bars with terraces located in the old harbour, that it's difficult to choose one. So just let yourself be guided by the rays of the sun and the available chairs. It's one of the busier locations in Rotterdam, so it's a good spot for people watching from early in the morning till late in the evening.

139 SOIF

Mathenesserdijk 438
West ⑥
+31 (0)10 476 74 36
soif.nl

Soif is a down to earth cafe-restaurant with a fantastic location: in historic Delfshaven, next to Lage Erf Bridge. On summer evenings, the terrace on the floating pontoon is a fabulous place to have dinner. Between the grape vine and olive trees and with a view over the River Schie you'll instantly feel as if you're on holiday far far away.

140 WESTKOP

Museumpark 35
Centre West ①
+31 (0)10 203 88 85
dewestkop.nl

Westkop is wedged between Het Nieuwe Instituut Museum and the iconic Museum Depot Boijmans Van Beuningen with its mirrors that reflect the city's skyline. The wide and sunny terrace is situated next to the pond and has great views. The bar serves a wide selection of beers and pizzas.

5 of the best
LOCAL BREWERIES

---

141 STADSHAVEN BROUWERIJ
Galileïstraat 24
West ⑥
+31 (0)10 307 68 38
stadshavenbrouwerij.nl

The Merwe-Vierhavens (or 'M4H') harbour district is becoming a vibrant new part of town. One reason to visit is the brewery annex Stadshaven gastropub that's located in an old fruit warehouse. It has a selection of homemade beers (from classics to fruity experimental brews), as well as a nice waterfront patio.

142 VET & LAZY
AT: BLUECITY
Maasboulevard 100
Centre East ②
lazy.vet

'Every brewer dreams of becoming fat and lazy', hence the name of this beer brewed at BlueCity. They have a lager, IPA and funky brews like Je Moeder (Your Mother), a triple with hibiscus and elderflower. The brewery is only open for group visits (min. 10 persons), but you'll find their beers all over town and occasionally at their own pop-up bar.

143 BROUWERIJ NOORDT
Zaagmolenkade 46
North ③
+31 (0)10 223 05 66
brouwerijnoordt.nl

A light and spacious brewery with large gleaming coppers and a taproom and store out front. Brouwerij Noordt is located in a former fire station in the up-and-coming Noord district. Try a blond or dark beer, a triple or saison.

144 KAAPSE BROUWERS
Keilestraat 9-F
West ⑥
+31 (0)6 184 177 73
kaapsebrouwers.nl

Kaapse Brouwers gives traditional beers, like IPAs, ales, bitters and stouts a modern twist and typical Rotterdam names such as Carrie, Harry, Karel and Gozer. Taste it all at Kaapse Maria, their own stylish but cosy bar at Mauritsweg 51. Or visit Kaapse Will'ns, their latest addition at Nieuwe Binnenweg.

145 DE PELGRIM
Aelbrechtskolk 12
West ⑥
+31 (0)10 477 11 89
pelgrimbier.nl

There wasn't a brewery left in the middle of the 1990s, when De Pelgrim was founded. Other new breweries followed in recent years. De Pelgrim's speciality beers are also used as an ingredient in the food that's served in the restaurant. The beer menu contains a steam beer and a triple as well as a variety of seasonal and experimental beers.

143 BROUWERIJ NOORDT

The 5

COSIEST CAFES

---

146 **TECH NOIR**
AT: 42WORKSPACE
Schiedamse Vest 154
Centre West ①
+31 (0)6 532 428 12
tech-noir.nl

While 'cosy' is not the first word that comes to mind when you think of Terminator, the 1984 film with Arnold Schwarzenegger, Tech Noir definitely has a homey eighties touch. Named after the bar in this film, it serves everything from coffee to cocktails and tasty American-inspired food in a bright neon-coloured interior.

147 **DE BALLENTENT**
Parkkade 1
Centre West ①
+31 (0)10 436 04 62
deballentent.nl

This used to be a customs' office and a dockworkers' hang-out, but now De Ballentent is a welcoming harbour cafe with fantastic views and waiters dressed in black and white. On the menu is classic cafe fare like *uitsmijter* (fried eggs), steak frites, and their award-winning meatballs.

148 CROOS

Exercitiestraat 2
Northeast ④
+31 (0)10 341 19 49
croosrotterdam.nl

This is truly a living room for old and new Crooswijk inhabitants, and for visitors of course. Meet here for a good cup of coffee, homemade pies and for alcoholic beverages and a plate full of snacks later in the day. There are separate places for working, a play area for kids, there's music on Sundays and changing art exhibitions.

149 SIJF

Oude Binnenweg 115
Centre West ①
+31 (0)10 433 26 10
sijf.nl

Sijf is one of those bars with a good crowd on a Friday evening, from office workers in suits to students and old regulars. Besides serving an excellent satay and other savoury bar food, they have an extensive beer menu, on which local breweries are well-represented. There's regular live music to go with your beer.

150 PROEFLOKAAL DE RIDDERT

Mauritsweg 28
Centre West ①
+31 (0)10 226 10 68
riddert.nl

This small cafe is a cross between a brown bar, a speciality beer cafe and a rock den. It's teeny-tiny, pitch-dark and extremely cosy. The beer list is long, the music alternative. In summer, the terrace expands across the parking spaces in front of the entrance.

The 5 best
WINE BARS

---

151 WIJNBAR HET EIGENDOM

**Witte de With-
straat 45-B
Centre West** ⓘ
+31 (0)10 413 79 62
heteigendom.nl

A lively and crowded wine bar with an excellent selection of over 130 old and new world wines. Have a small bite to eat with your glass of red, white or rosé. Or, if you manage to grab a table, you can also get a more substantial seven-course tasting menu with paired wines.

152 VINEUM

**Eendrachtsweg 23
Centre West** ⓘ
+31 (0)10 720 09 66
vineum.nl

A restaurant and wine bar with an award-winning 'world class' wine list. Owner David van Steenderen is a sommelier and he takes his wine seriously: old world wines are served in crystal glasses at the right temperature. The cafe and wine bar are on the ground floor, the restaurant is on the first floor. Weather permitting, try to get a table in the fabulous vine covered inner courtyard.

153 NOSTRA

Van Oldenbarnevelt-
straat 127-A
Centre West ①
+31 (0)10 213 22 22
nostra-rotterdam.nl

Sure you've heard of high tea, but have you ever tried high wining? At Nostra you can enjoy a table full of delicious savoury snacks paired with two glasses of wine (reserve ahead). Nostra has a concise, but carefully curated wine list and a very extensive and tasty lunch menu, so you won't leave the place feeling tipsy.

154 PRÊT À BOIRE

Bloemfontein-
straat 78-C
South ⑤
+31 (0)6 505 206 18
pretaboire.nl

Pretorialaan is the gateway to the Afrikaanderwijk, a lively and multicultural neighbourhood on the south bank of the river. Prêt à Boire (ready to drink) is specialised in natural wines, but you can also go there for coffee and small snacks.

155 WIJNBAR JANSSEN EN VAN DIJK

Westewagenstraat 58
Centre East ①
+31 (0)10 413 11 44
*wijnbarjanssen
envandijk.nl*

The owners, Albert van Dijk and Saraja Janssen, succeeded in making their wine bar feel like a home away from home. Cosy, like your favourite winter coat. They have a small but good selection of French wine and meat, fish or cheese dishes to accompany your glass of choice.

The 5 most
CLASSY CAFES

---

156 YOLO

**Admiraliteits-
straat 17-B**
Northeast ④
+31 (0)10 414 27 95
restaurant-yolo.com

A peacock with long flowing tail feathers reigns supremely over this fantastically decorated bar with an even better location. Drink your Golddigger or Naughty Schoolgirl cocktail while enjoying views of the marina. Even the food is classy and delicate here, including tiny Wagyu beef burgers or seared tuna on a skewer.

157 CAFÉ DE OUWEHOER

157 CAFÉ DE OUWEHOER
Delistraat 36-C
South ⑤
+31 (0)10 486 52 53
cafedeouwehoer.nl

Café De Ouwehoer honours the raucous history of Katendrecht: it used to have the highest concentration of sailors, bars and prostitutes in Rotterdam. The tastefully executed interior is burlesque with lots of red velvet and naked busts. It's a warm and inviting stylish bar with a very good whisky selection.

158 LOOS
AT: ATLANTIC HUIS
Westplein 51
Centre West ①
+31 (0)10 411 77 23
loos-rotterdam.nl

Located on the corner of the fabulous Atlantic House (an impressive brick building in art deco style) and with a view of the historical Veerhaven, this is one of the best places to enjoy a cup of coffee or a glass of Chardonnay. Loos is a classic grand cafe and has an equally classic menu.

159 BAR PANENKA
Eendrachtsweg 25
Centre West ①
+31 (0)10 845 98 99
panenkarotterdam.com

More gentlemen's club than sport canteen, this is the most stylish sports bar you're likely to find. They even have a private skybox. Watch a football game with your friends and enjoy a nice glass of beer and a plate of porchetta or hot wings.

160 NIEUW ROTTERDAMS CAFE
Witte de Withstraat 63
Centre West ①
+31 (0)10 414 41 88
nieuwrotterdams cafe.nl

A spacious grand cafe with metropolitan allure that's named after the newspaper *(NRC)* that used to be located here. Recline in comfortable design chairs for a late afternoon drink (or two) and a snack. Downstairs is the club area that's open till late in the weekend. They have a very nice terrace out front as well, a prime spot in bustling Witte de Withstraat.

THEATER WALHALLA

35 PLACES
TO GO OUT

The 5 best
JAZZ VENUES

---

161 BIRD

Raampoortstraat 24
North ③
+31 (0)10 737 11 54
bird-rotterdam.nl

Everything in this venue breathes jazz. Expect an eclectic mix of jazz, hip-hop, soul and dance. Or, as the man who came up with the plans for the venue said: 'I'm of the generation that got into jazz through hip-hop.' The best place to start your jazz night is in Bird's restaurant, which serves excellent Neapolitan brick-oven pizzas.

162 DIZZY

's-Gravendijkwal 127
West ⑥
+31 (0)10 477 30 14
dizzy.nl

Rotterdam has a dynamic jazz history and Dizzy has played a central part in it. The club opened in 1977 and has welcomed artists like George Coleman and Lee Konitz. And Chet Baker, who gave a surprise performance here just days before he died. There are concerts several nights a week. Check the website, or drop in for a drink or a bite and see what happens.

163 DE MACHINIST

Willem Buytewech-
straat 45
West ⑥
+31 (0)10 477 57 00
demachinist.nl

This massive building in Delfshaven used to be the college for shipping and transport. Here trainees once got on-the-job training in smithing and machine operations. The bar used to be the boiler room. From October to March, free jazz concerts are organised here every Sunday at 3 pm.

164 CAFÉ LABRU

Hartmansstraat 18-A
Centre East ②
+31 (0)10 737 12 05

Fashionable but cosy Café LaBru has a tiny stage where weekly jazz concerts (and also other types of concerts) are organised. The menu contains a good selection of whiskies, cocktails and tasty finger food.

165 NORTH SEA ROUND TOWN

AT: VARIOUS LOCATIONS
northsearoundtown.nl

The three-day North Sea Jazz festival in early July is one of the most established jazz festivals in the world. Less well-known is its little brother North Sea Round Town. This 'fringe festival' is a prelude to the 'real' festival. It lasts for two weeks, with hundreds of concerts at dozens of locations (from well-known music venues, to a swimming pool or a hospital).

The 5 best places to listen to
CLASSICAL MUSIC

---

166 LAURENSKERK

Grotekerkplein 27
Centre East ②
+31 (0)10 411 64 94
*laurenskerk
rotterdam.nl*

Laurenskerk programmes dozens of own productions and external acts every year. This 15th-century church also has the largest pipe organ of the country, which is used by many musicians who play here. A guide can take you to the top of the 65-metre church tower on Wednesdays and Saturdays (from April to October) to enjoy the view.

167 DE DOELEN

Schouwburgplein 50
Centre West ①
+31 (0)10 217 17 17
dedoelen.nl

Not many concert halls can say they have their own pipe organ. But there's much more to say about De Doelen, which has four concert halls and programmes about 600 classical, jazz and world music concerts every year, making it the second largest classical music venue in the country. It's also the home base of the Rotterdam Philharmonic Orchestra.

168 BREEPLEINKERK

Van Malsenstraat 104
South ⑤
+31 (0)10 419 11 96
breepleinkerk.nl

A Jewish couple hid in the attic of this church during World War II, in a little space just behind the pipe organ. The woman even gave birth to a child here, with assistance from a resistance fighter. When visiting the church, make sure to check the website for scheduled classical concerts or come listen to the choral practice on Sunday afternoon.

169 O.

AT: VARIOUS LOCATIONS
+31 (0)10 436 60 70
o-festival.nl

Rotterdam is all about opera at the end of May. Numerous locations throughout the city participate in this ten-day-festival, which gives a diverse overview of contemporary opera and music theatre, and seeks to serve both seasoned opera lovers and people who are new to the genre.

170 HEERENHUYS CONCERTS

AT: DUDOK IN HET PARK
Baden Powelllaan 12
Centre West ①
+31 (0)10 290 84 44
*heerenhuys
kamerconcerten.nl*

On Sunday morning, you can enjoy acoustic concerts in the monumental 18th-century villa Het Heerenhuys, in the Park near the Euromast: classical music, jazz and light pop music. If you want, you can order breakfast served by brasserie Dudok together with your ticket through the website.

5 of the best places to enjoy
ALTERNATIVE MUSIC

171 ROTOWN

Nieuwe Binnenweg 19
Centre West ①
+31 (0)10 436 26 42
rotown.nl

Rotown has a variety of concerts, dance nights and other events scheduled on most days of the week, even on Monday nights. The venue's history goes back to 1987, when this former Chinese restaurant was turned into a small concert hall, restaurant and bar. Rotown has since welcomed bands like Bright Eyes, Catpower, and Franz Ferdinand.

172 V11 (VESSEL 11)

Wijnhaven 101
Centre East ②
+31 (0)10 840 47 30
vessel11.nl

You can enjoy an excellent lunch or meal in the cosy cabin of this flaming red light vessel from 1951, or enjoy a glass of their home-brewed ale on deck. V11 has its own concert programme, and also cooperates with Rotown. Concert and dance evenings are organised in the cargo hold.

173 GROUNDS

Pieter de Hooch-
weg 125
West ⑥
+31 (0)6 191 135 16
grounds.nu

This small music venue (capacity 200) hosts an eclectic mix of hip-hop and jazz acts from all over the world, but from Africa and Latin America in particular. A second location opened in a former school building at 's-Gravendijkwal.

174 BAROEG

Spinozaweg 300
South ⑤
+31 (0)10 432 57 35
baroeg.nl

This is the place to go for those who like it loud. Metalheads, hard rockers and punks from around the country know Baroeg for its wayward programming of 'hard alternative music'. Baroeg's history dates back to the early 1980s and it's still a venue for national and international bands that aren't invited to play elsewhere.

175 ANNABEL

Schiestraat 20
Centre West ①
+31 (0)6 382 391 53
(only Whatsapp)
annabel.nu

With enough room for 1500 visitors, Annabel is one of the biggest concert venues in Rotterdam. It has an industrial vibe that matches well with the surrounding Schieblock (a 'laboratory for urban development'). The venue specialises in urban music, but Annabel also has pop music and dance nights.

172 **V11 (VESSEL 11)**

5 of the best
CLUBS
in town

---

176 CLUB BIT

Keileweg 10-A
West ⑥
bit-ter.nl

A creative hotspot, a club where you can dance till the early morning, an eccentric safe space: Club BIT is all of it. As the night progresses, one DJ after another climbs the stage, playing a variety of musical styles. The artistic vibe of BIT is underlined by the fact that the building, a former brothel in the M4H harbour area, is owned by the artist Joep van Lieshout, who has his workshop next door.

177 MAASSILO

Maashaven Zuid-
zijde 1
South ⑤
+31 (0)10 476 24 52
maassilo.com

Beats echo against the massive concrete walls of this large industrial building in the southern harbour. Parts of the old grain silos are still visible from the ceiling, adding to the underground look and feel of this venue. The legendary (and very eccentric) Now&Wow parties are organised on Saturday nights.

178 SUPERDISCO

Schiedamse Vest 91
Centre West ⓘ
+31 (0)10 04 80 70
superdiscorotterdam.nl

From Wednesday till Saturday, the basement of Supermercado, a Mexican street food restaurant annex cocktail bar, changes into a steaming hot night club around midnight. You'll find a mixed crowd that won't leave until the early hours.

179 TOFFLER

Weena Zuid 33
Centre West ⓘ
toffler.nl

A hydraulic system changes the location of the stage depending on the time: small and cosy when it's still early, large when it gets crowded. The club is located in a former pedestrian tunnel and organises techno parties on Friday, Saturday and occasionally on Thursday nights.

180 CLUB VIBES

Westersingel 50-A
Centre West ⓘ
+31 (0)10 200 29 37
clubvibes.nl

This tiny, intimate club opens from Wednesday to Saturday from around 11 pm till the early morning. Check the calendar for other dance nights or occasional concerts. Expect a surprising mix of recent pop hits and golden oldies.

The 5 coolest
LATE NIGHT BARS

181 **CAFÉ KEERWEER**
Keerweer 14 (day)
1e Westblaakhof
(night)
Centre West ①
+31 (0)10 413 12 17
keerweer.nl

From 1 am onwards, the entrance of Café KeerWeer closes and visitors are asked to enter through the back door at 1e Westblaakhof. Although a popular hang-out for the Rotterdam gay scene, you'll encounter many heterosexual men and women here as well. KeerWeer is open till 6 am every day of the week, so things gets livelier as the night progresses.

182 **CAFÉ DE ZONDEBOK & 'T ZWARTESCHAAP**
Witte de With-
straat 96
Centre West ①
+31 (0)10 213 63 00

The unpronounceable name of this quirky 'new style brown bar' means 'the scapegoat and the black sheep'. It stays open till 5 am from Friday to Sunday and till 4 am on other days. Expect an alternative music selection that goes from roaring guitars, deejays mixing blues and soul tunes, and pumping electro beats.

183 BAR3

Nieuwe Binnen-
weg 17
Centre West ①
bar3.nl

This alternative rock cafe is located next to its little sister Rotown, the concert venue at Nieuwe Binnenweg. It's the place to be for those who want to bounce away to rock music till late (or for people-watching from the terrace on this ever-lively street). Concerts and other events are organised here from time to time.

184 BONAPARTE

Nieuwe Binnen-
weg 117-A
Centre West ①
cafe-bonaparte.
business.site

If you really don't want to go home, go to Bonaparte. In this small and cosy gay and drag night cafe the vibe is always good and there are singalongs to keep you going until the small hours of the morning. Because at Bonaparte, time is relative. So, don't be surprised to hear the birds singing once you've finally decided to call it a night.

185 DE WITTE AAP

Witte de With-
straat 78
Centre East ②
+31 (0)10 414 95 65
dewitteaap.nl

The patio of De Witte Aap ('the white monkey') opens around noon, and is a nice place to observe passers-by on the arty Witte de Withstraat. But this dark and traditional looking bar really wakes up at night. It's open seven days a week till the early hours.

The 5 best places for
THEATRE

186 THEATER ROTTERDAM SCHOUWBURG

Schouwburgplein 25
Centre West ①
+31 (0)10 411 81 10
theaterrotterdam.nl

Theater Rotterdam is both the biggest theatre venue in the city and a major theatre production house. There are two locations: the theatre at Schouwburgplein is the main venue, a smaller venue is located in the Witte de With area (William Boothlaan 8). The programme aims to be unconventional and thought-provoking, and offers plenty of room for emerging talent.

187 THEATER WALHALLA

Sumatraweg 9-11
South ⑤
+31 (0)10 215 21 34
theaterwalhalla.nl

People were once dancing through the night to the sounds of a barrel organ in Dancing Walhalla. A grassroots initiative led to the establishment of a small theatre here, in 2008. An appealing programme with performances, cabaret and music for all ages and by talented artists resulted in an expansion across the street, where an extra hall and restaurant were built in the former harbour workers' canteen.

188 COMEDY CLUB HAUG

Boompjeskade 11
Centre East ②
+31 (0)6 218 674 24
comedyclubhaug.com

The founders of this intimate comedy club pulled quite a stunt when they had the world-famous comedian Louis C.K. perform on their very first night in 2019. Shows are scheduled on several evenings throughout the week, both in Dutch and English. Haug also has a waterfront terrace that offers a great view on the three iconic bridges of Rotterdam.

189 MAASPODIUM

St. Jobsweg 3
West ⑥
+31 (0)10 707 04 39
maastd.nl

Children, teenagers and adolescents are the main audience of this family theatre, which is run by several theatre groups that focus on youth theatre. Expect a wide variety of plays, dance and music performances, and location-specific theatre. Parents are invited to join.

190 OUDE LUXOR THEATER

Kruiskade 10
Centre West ①
+31 (0)10 484 33 33
luxortheater.nl

Built as an art deco-style cinema in 1917, Het Oude Luxor became the city's central place for accessible theatre in the decades that followed. The programming now includes plays, cabaret and music (theatre). A second and larger location, Het Nieuwe Luxor, opened in 2001 at Kop van Zuid (Posthumalaan 1). Visit the website for the programme of both locations.

The 5 best
CINEMAS

---

191 LANTARENVENSTER

Otto Reuchlin-
weg 996
South ⑤
+31 (0)10 277 22 77
lantarenvenster.nl

For decades, LantarenVenster was the city's cinematic heart. This didn't change when they moved to their current location in Kop van Zuid. The programme includes arthouse movies, world cinema, classics and special programmes for children. There's also a restaurant and regular jazz and world music concerts.

193 CINERAMA

192 KINO

Gouvernestraat 129
Centre West ①
+31 (0)10 268 11 60
kinorotterdam.nl

KINO screens a pleasant mix of arthouse films, bigger titles and self-curated themed screenings. The bar is dotted with hidden movie references, making it the perfect spot to discuss the film you've just watched. The building's cinematographic history goes back to the 1940s and was also the birthplace of the International Filmfestival Rotterdam.

193 CINERAMA

Westblaak 18
Centre West ①
+31 (0)10 411 53 00
cineramabios.nl

The films shown in Cinerama range from, as they like to describe it, 'arthouse to Hollywood' and everything in between. Have a look at the website for occasional special screenings.

194 CINENOORD

AT: STUDIO DE BAKKERIJ
Bergweg 283
North ③
+31 (0)6 477 773 47
cinenoord.nl

This cinema is an initiative of some locals in Rotterdam North. Films are screened on Thursday nights and teen films on Wednesday afternoons. Every screening is preceded by a brief introduction and a short movie made by a Rotterdam director.

195 PATHÉ SCHOUWBURGPLEIN

Schouwburgplein 101
Centre West ①
pathe.nl

This is by far the largest cinema in the city centre, with 7 screens, about 2000 seats and one of the few IMAX cinemas in the country. Here you can see all the latest blockbusters and Hollywood flicks. Another Pathé branch is located at Feyenoord football stadium.

STEK

75 PLACES
TO GO SHOPPING

———

The 5 best
SHOPPING STREETS

196 NIEUWE BINNENWEG
Centre West ①

Once known for its many bars, the long and winding Nieuwe Binnenweg is now Rotterdam's most diverse and lively shopping street with many independent retailers. From record shops, barbers, shoe stores and antiques to lunch rooms, exotic restaurants and brown cafes. Follow this street to the end, and you'll arrive in historic Delfshaven.

197 ZWAANSHALS
North ③

A thorough revamp turned Zwaanshals (swan neck) into a vibrant, rejuvenated area bursting with small speciality shops, vintage clothing, furniture, cosy cafes and affordable restaurants. If you have enough time, explore nearby Zaagmolenkade and Zwart Janstraat as well.

198 PANNEKOEKSTRAAT / BOTERSLOOT

Centre East ②

These two little streets benefited from the increasing rents on the more upscale Meent. It meant that the smaller and more interesting independent retailers relocated to Pannekoekstraat and Botersloot. You'll find (vintage) clothing shops, a magnificent children's book shop, antiques and some of the most laidback cafes and restaurants here.

199 HOFBOGEN

Raampoortstraat /
Vijverhofstraat /
Voorburgstraat
North ③
hofbogen.nl

In recent years a surprising number of shops and restaurants have established themselves in the renovated arcs of this disused railway line. From coffee roasters to artisanal bakeries, and from interior design shops to record stores. Tired of shopping? Find somewhere to sit in one of the many hip restaurants or espresso bars.

200 WITTE DE WITHSTRAAT

Centre West ①

In the 1980s Witte de Withstraat was rundown and somewhat of a no-go area. That's hard to believe now, as it is definitely Rotterdam's most vibrant street. It hums with life well into the night. In between the many trendy cafes and delicious eateries from around the world, you'll find design stores, galleries and vintage clothing shops. Don't forget the side streets.

The 5 best

INDEPENDENT

BOOKSTORES

---

201 BOEKHANDEL V/H VAN GENNEP

Oude Binnen-
weg 131-B
Centre West ⓘ
+31 (0)10 433 05 92
boekhandel
vangennep.nl

For about half a century, Van Gennep has been the go-to independent bookstore. More than just a shop, it's a meeting place for lovers of literature, children's books, photography, design and cookbooks. There are regular in-store book presentations and readings.

202 DONNER

Coolsingel 129
Centre West ⓘ
+31 (0)10 413 20 70
donner.nl

This formidable and well-stocked bookstore that was once the pride of Rotterdam was swallowed up by a big chain that unfortunately went bankrupt in 2014. Luckily, Donner was rescued by a successful crowdfunding campaign that raised 250.000 euros. It is now located in an impressive and entirely renovated former bank building. Don't miss the decorated window near the entrance, designed by mid-century glass artist Andries Copier.

203 NAI BOOKSELLERS
AT: HET NIEUWE INSTITUUT
Museumpark 25
Centre West ①
+31 (0)10 440 12 03
www.naibooksellers.nl

Het Nieuwe Instituut is home to a well-stocked independent bookstore with the latest publications on architecture, urban planning and design. They also have a good selection of city and architecture guidebooks. But be warned: many of the books have very enticing designs and are hard to put down once you pick them up.

204 BOSCH EN DE JONG
AT: FENIX FOOD FACTORY
Nico Koomans-kade 1025
South ⑤
+31 (0)6 287 002 81
boschendejong.nl

Eelkje and Folco run their compact and cosy bookshop Bosch en De Jong inside the Fenix Food Factory. On offer is the latest in literature in English and Dutch, children's books, graphic novels, cookbooks and a good selection of books on Rotterdam. The owners are always willing to share their reading tips and give advice.

205 OOSTERBOEKHANDEL J. AMESZ
Voorschoter-laan 145-A
Northeast ④
+31 (0)10 412 36 38

This is a bookstore like a bookstore is supposed to be, with three storeys stacked full of books, and three friendly ladies who can tell you all about the books they sell. This bookstore has been around since 1886 and is known for its personal touch. If you come more than once, the personnel will give you personalised advice and call you by name.

5 stylish
DESIGNERS
from Rotterdam

---

206 CLAN DE BANLIEUE

Zaagmolendrift 53
North ③
+31 (0)10 840 02 38
clandebanlieue.com

Banlieue spread around Rotterdam like wildfire: it's hard to walk around this city without spotting someone who is wearing (part of) their tracksuits. What started as a school project in 2014 has become a professional streetwear label, luckily still rooted in Rotterdam, with its own store.

207 DAISY KROON

1e Pijnacker-
straat 123-B
North ③
+31 (0)6 471 981 88
daisykroon.com

She graduated with honours from the Willem de Kooning Academy in 2007 and since then has been building a steady reputation with clean aesthetics and wearable fashion. Her work has attracted international attention and resulted in an exhibition in the Museum Boijmans Van Beuningen. Visit Daisy Kroon's shop and studio on the corner of lovely Branco square.

208 CHARLOTTE WOONING

Hoogstraat 8-A
Centre East ②
+31 (0)10 243 03 15
charlottewooning.com

In her shop in Hoogstraat – 'Every day is a day to be beautiful' – Charlotte Wooning sells her own jewellery designs. Wooning, a graduate of Rotterdam's Willem de Kooning Academy, sets herself apart with refined, subtle and elegant pieces of jewellery made with sterling silver, gold and gemstones.

209 JOLINE JOLINK

Nieuwe Binnen-
weg 82
Centre West ①
+31 (0)10 737 10 83
jolinejolink.com

Joline Jolink studied in Arnhem, worked in New York and opened her first shop in Amsterdam, but a few years ago, she relocated her home and store to Rotterdam. Now she designs and develops all her products in her own studio in Rotterdam. Her collection is inspired by strong, real women. The clothes are timeless and versatile.

210 A. BRANDSMA

Delftseplein 36
Centre East ②
a-brandsma.com

Clean lines, neat silhouettes and colourful fabrics define Amber Brandsma's fashion label. Embracing slow fashion, she produces handmade quality items that are made to last and are easy to wear. Visit her website or the Slowdown Store at Burgemeester Meineszplein.

The 5 best places to buy
DESIGNER CLOTHES

211 MOSTERT & VAN LEEUWEN

Van Oldenbarnevelt-
straat 131
Centre East ②
+31 (0)10 404 80 04
mostertvanleeuwen.nl

Chic, with a touch of casual, that's what owners Hugo Mostert and Sander van Leeuwen want their two stores to be. They sell classic and fashion-forward womenswear. Expect fashion by Stella McCartney, Nina Ricci and Dries van Noten, as well as accessories such as jewellery and bags.

212 NXA

Pannekoekstraat 62-A
Centre East ②
+31 (0)6 391 939 32
newxarchive.com

In his light-filled and accessible shop, Nen Xavier sells a curated collection of upcoming brands from around the world. Nen has a refreshing take on fashion, offering a collection that is, in his own words, "ageless, timeless, genderless".

213 BOHEMIAN BY JIBODH

Pannekoekstraat 48-A
Centre East ②
+31 (0)10 737 15 68
bohemianrotterdam.nl

Bohemian by Jibodh sells casual chic Scandinavian, Italian and Rotterdam brands, among others, always stocking the latest trends. The stylishly decorated shop is owned by two brothers who take pride in giving personal and honest advice.

214 MARGREETH OLSTHOORN

Wilhelminakade 52
South ⑤
+31 (0)10 282 75 42
shop.margreeth
olsthoorn.nl

In her shop in a former warehouse at Kop van Zuid, designer and fashion curator Margreeth Olsthoorn combines high-end fashion with avant-garde art and conceptual design. She sells men's and women's clothing by brands such as Rick Owens, Henrik Vibskov, Viktor&Rolf and Birgitte Herskind.

215 OBJET TROUVÉ

Pannekoekstraat 44-A
Centre East ②
+31 (0)10 737 14 44
objet-trouve.nl

Sisters Josje and Floor Theuns wanted to bring some Parisian elegance and Scandinavian cool to Rotterdam. In their beautiful minimalist store, they sell clothing by Ulla Johnson, Citizens of Humanity and their in-house line ICONS, as well as scarves by Faliero Sarti and jewellery by Wouters & Hendrix.

211 MOSTERT & VAN LEEUWEN

5 places to buy
SPECIAL SHOES

216 WOEI

Hoogstraat 44-A
Centre East ②
+31 (0)10 404 85 31
woei-webshop.nl

Woei is heaven for sneaker aficionados. Fans have been known to camp in front of the store to get their hands on a new limited edition sneaker or to be the first to browse through the Woei Sale. Owner Woei Tjin is a big sneaker fan and owns more than 400 pairs himself. He sells an impressive collection of Nikes, but also Karhu, Adidas, New Balance and Saucony sneakers.

217 MASCOLORI

Nieuwe Binnen-
weg 116
Centre West ①
+31 (0)10 223 05 35
www.mascolori.nl

Stylish and rebellious in one, Mascolori shoes are bold and colourful, and will definitely allow you to make an entrance. Some of the designs are collaborations with artists, like the Rotterdam shoes and socks by outsider artist Laan Irodjojo. There are changing exhibitions and performances in the store, and you can enjoy an espresso, wine or *jenever* while browsing.

218 VAN DEN ASSEM

Aert van Nes-
straat 38-50
Centre West ①
+31 (0)10 411 21 11
assem.nl

For over 100 years this family business has been holding quality and good service in high esteem. Van den Assem is the biggest and best organised shoe store of Rotterdam, selling pumps, brogues, boots, ballerinas, sneakers and slippers. They carry a wide range of brands in men's, women's and children's shoes.

219 CALAND/SCHOEN

Nieuwe Binnenweg 14
Centre West ①
+31 (0)10 436 63 17
groteschoenen.nl

Having trouble finding fashionable shoes in your size? Try Caland/Schoen, which sells women's shoes in sizes 37 through 46 and men's shoes sizes 46-52. This business, which is over 100 years old, is located in a stylishly decorated shop with changing art exhibitions. The personnel will happily help you find a perfect fit.

220 VICO

Goudsesingel 60
Centre East ②
+31 (0)10 846 02 40
vico-movement.com

Vicus means 'on the street' or 'in the neighbourhood' in Latin; places, in short, where one wears sporty footwear. Vico sells elegant sneakers for men and women with an international twist. Their shoes are designed in Italy, handmade in Portugal from quality European leather, and sold in Rotterdam.

5 great shops to buy
VINTAGE CLOTHING

221 VON DEUX VINTAGE

Goudsesingel 69
Centre East ②
von-deux.com

Because the wares are conveniently sorted
by colour, you can easily find that perfect
item to complement your wardrobe at
Von Deux Vintage. Out of inspiration?
Owner Rosanne models original looks
on Instagram and will gladly advise you.

222 DEARHUNTER VINTAGE

222 DEARHUNTER VINTAGE

Eendrachtsweg 55-A
Centre West ①
+31 (0)6 288 039 56
dearhunter.fresh.li

Dearhunter doesn't sell your typical knitted sweaters or band T-shirts with holes in them. This shop sells high fashion items for dressing up every day and rocking that sidewalk. Think Burberry trench coats, Versace pants, sequined tops and bow ties.

223 SWEET REBELS

Schiedamse Vest 89-B
Centre West ①
+31 (0)6 527 167 62
sweet-rebels.com

The owner Mitzy has a passion for vintage fashion. Her small but cosy shop is located just off Witte de Withstraat. She'll give you weekly updates of new clothing for sale on the Sweet Rebels' Facebook page. Expect a combination of high-end fashion finds, bold and colourful showpieces and original accessories.

224 BOBBY PIN BOUTIQUE

Rodenburgstraat 59
North ③
+31 (0)6 526 485 46
bobbypinboutique.nl

Bobby Pin collects vintage from all over the world, specialising in 1930s and 1940s clothing, but their collection also includes items up to the 60s. They have a very good selection of men's clothing as well. Shop online, or make an appointment to give yourself plenty of time to browse the collection and try on their vintage gems.

225 BETJE KRUL VINTAGE

Zwaanshals 344
North ③

For colourful and fun dresses, skirts, jumpsuits and playsuits, Betje Krul is definitely the place to go. Marcella, the warm and welcoming owner who cherishes her happy customers, will give you honest and good advice.

The 5 most special
CONCEPT STORES

226 SWAN MARKET

Oude Binnenweg 137
Centre West ①
+31 (0)10 737 07 08
swanmarket.nl

The Swan Market is the place for creative Rotterdammers to peddle their wares. In addition to the recurring open-air Swan Market that takes place in different locations, there is now a physical store as well. Browse two floors full of handmade clothing, accessories and interior design items, made or selected by some 20 different designers.

227 KEET

Oppert 2-A
Centre East ②
+31 (0)10 210 54 33
keetrotterdam.nl

Keet provides a platform for creative entrepreneurs and webshop owners. They can rent a little piece of the store and sell their ware. Think interior decoration, jewellery and an endless array of perfect gifts.

228 VOORLOPIG

Nieuwe Binnen-
weg 165
Centre West ①
+31 (0)6 398 402 17
voorlopig
conceptstore.com

It's hard to walk by this eccentric department store on the Nieuwe Binnenweg without stopping to look at the enticing window display. Walk in and get lost in this *wunderkammer* full of statuettes, porcelain, earthenware, postcards, books, and all other things you didn't know you needed until visiting Voorlopig.

229 NISHI MARKET

Meent 7-9
Centre East ②
+31 (0)10 314 11 28
nishimarket.com

The interior is so pink, you could easily mistake this place for a candy shop. But Nishi Market is actually a Japanese concept store, decorated in an extremely cute and sweet Kawaii style. Nishi sells clothing and accessories, stationery, books on and from Japan, beauty products, homeware, snacks and (equally colourful) bubble teas.

230 RUMOURS [CONCEPT] STORE

Lusthofstraat 57
Northeast ④
+31 (0)10 303 19 23
rumoursconceptstore.nl

A carefully curated concept store where there's always something new to look at. From fashion, garden decoration and homeware to personal care items and accessories. The store is located at Lusthofstraat, the main shopping street in the elegant Kralingen district.

The 5 best
BARBER SHOPS

───────────

231 SCHOREM

Nieuwe Binnen-
weg 104
Centre West ①
+31 (0)10 241 03 09
schorembarbier.nl

Schorem (scumbag) single-handedly made old-fashioned barbershops cool again. Men flock here from all over the globe to get a perfectly pomaded pompadour, a wet towel shave, and to have a drink and a chat. Schorem even started their own training academy.

232 NEW YORK BARBERSHOP

AT: HOTEL NEW YORK
Koninginnenhoofd 1
South ⑤
+31 (0)10 485 31 96
newyorkbarbershop.nl

Way ahead of the current barbershop hype, this store in the basement of Hotel New York opened in 1884 and has been a family business ever since. Treat yourself to a 'hot towel, straight razor, wet shave', or have your beard trimmed and your moustache curled in this grand and luxurious barbershop.

233 MUDLY'S BARBERSHOP

Nieuwe Binnen-
weg 200-B
West ⑥
+31 (0)10 244 95 23
mudlysbarbershop.nl

Thomas and his crew give modern haircuts in a classic fifties American barbershop setting. Their repertoire includes tight bobs, multi-coloured mohawks, perfectly trimmed beards and perky quiffs.

234 LA FEE VERTE BEAUTY PARLOUR

Zwaanshals 276-B
North ③
+31 (0)6 244 954 24
lafeeverte.nl

Entering La Fee Verte is like stepping into a vintage lover's living room instead of a hairdresser's. When the green fairy *(la fee verte)* aka Jerry Gardenier waves her magic wand you'll leave the shop feeling like a new human being. She also organises occasional workshops about vintage hairstyles.

235 ROTTERDAM BARBERS

Pijnackerplein 1-A
North ③
+31 (0)10 236 11 47
rotterdambarbers.com

Coos Ravelo's barber shop is located on a corner at Pijnackerplein, a charming little neighbourhood square in the northern part of town. Coos had years of experience as a barber before he opened his own shop some years ago. He'll give you a traditional and stylish haircut, trim your beard, perfect your stubble or shave you perfectly bald, if that's your thing.

232 NEW YORK BARBERSHOP

The 5 best
RECORD SHOPS

236 DE PLAATBOEF
Nieuwe Binnen-
weg 81-A
Centre West ①
+31 (0)10 436 58 73
plaatboef.nl

This is the best place to go to if you're looking for secondhand CDS, DVDS and vinyl. They also have seven inch singles and 78s, ask for those if you're interested. De Plaatboef has over 200 square metres filled to the brim with music, not only used music, but new as well. They regularly host in store concerts.

238 DEMONFUZZ RECORDS

237 VELVET MUSIC

Oude Binnen-
weg 121-A
Centre West ⓘ
+31 (0)10 413 44 23
velvetmusic.nl

What you can't do on the Internet, you can do at Velvet Music: hold and smell records and talk endlessly with the very knowledgeable staff. A lot of people come here not only to browse and buy CDS and vinyl, but also to have a chat with Manfred, who has been selling records here since 1990.

238 DEMONFUZZ RECORDS

Nieuwe Binnen-
weg 86
Centre West ⓘ
+31 (0)10 436 59 99
demonfuzz.com

At Demonfuzz you'll find that obscure reggae LP, the newest hip-hop release or that rock classic you were looking for. You can easily spend a few hours here. It's a favourite haunt of DJS from all around the world.

239 VINYLSPOT

Josephstraat 162
Centre West ⓘ
+31 (0)10 707 07 15
vinylspot.nl

Rotterdam has a strong jazz tradition and if you're looking for a jazz record that's hard to find, try Vinylspot. The shop's owner, Lex, is a bottomless pit when it comes to musical knowledge and willingly hands out advice. His shop is bright and well-organised. Besides vinyl he also sells record players.

240 CLONE RECORDS

Raampoortstraat 12
North ③
+31 (0)10 436 95 06
clone.nl

Clone Records was founded in the nineties and quickly gained a reputation in house music and experimental/underground electronic dance music. Nowadays, they sell jazz, funk, soul and even classical music in their shop located under a former railway viaduct. Clone is not only a record shop, but a label and distributor as well.

5 of the most outstanding
SPECIALITY SHOPS

241 VAN DALEN CIGARS

Pannekoek-
straat 28-A
Centre East ②
+31 (0)10 413 16 99
sigaren.com

A few years ago, Van Dalen left the Meent to move into this bigger and better shop just a few blocks away. This family owned store sells handmade cigars and smoker's requisites. Their classy smoker's lounge is especially enticing (even to non-smokers).

242 KOOKPUNT

Noordplein 29
North ③
+31 (0)10 443 10 75
kookpunt.nl

Whether you're looking for kitchen utensils or a specific appliance, this 4000-square-metre emporium has it all. Kookpunt has anything from carving knives to blenders, from barbecues to cookbooks and even stoves and espresso machines. They sell, but also repair.

243 SCRAP

Schoterbosstraat 6-C
North ③
+31 (0)6 285 675 35
scrapxl.nl

Make art, not waste. Scrap collects industrial leftovers from car tires, paint and wool to bottles, buttons, flags and plastic bits. Just walking through the store feels like an exciting expedition. Scrap is popular with artists, hobbyists and schools. They organise creative workshops and children's parties as well.

244 STRIPWINKEL YENDOR

Korte Hoogstraat 16
Centre East ②
+31 (0)10 433 17 10
yendor.nl

Just off the busy Hoogstraat shopping street you'll find this calm oasis filled with comic books, graphic novels and paraphernalia like T-shirts and mugs. You can browse this spacious and well-sorted shop for hours. Yendor, which opened in 1977, is the oldest comic book store in town.

245 WHISKYBASE

Zwaanshals 530
North ③
+31 (0)10 753 17 43
whiskybase.com

Heaven for whisky lovers, this shop sells a lot of independent bottlers and original bottlings from Ireland, Scotland, the United States, and even India, Japan, and Switzerland. They also have their own label: Archives. Owners Menno and Cees-Jan can tell you all about the different kinds. They organise monthly tastings.

241 VAN DALEN CIGARS

The 5 best places for hunting
ANTIQUES and
CURIOSITIES

246 FITZROY & EVEREST 'GENTLEMEN'S ANTIQUES'

Vredehofstraat 54-B
North ③
+31 (0)10 411 88 01
fitzroy-everest.nl

A treasure trove for real English gentlemen with a love of antiques. Olivier van Schaik sells old leather suitcases, cabin trunks, binocular cases, globes, original sports prints, and lots of sports accessories like gloves, shoes, leather footballs, wooden tennis rackets and antique golf clubs. A marvellous shop to browse and admire the style and class of bygone times.

247 VINTAGE AAN DE ROTTE

Zwaanshals 468
North ③
+31 (0)6 428 157 66
vintagerotterdam.nl

At the age of 20, Marga started collecting vases and tableware from the 1960s. Her scope later expanded to everything mid-century: lamps, furniture, ceramics and other objects. She now has her own shop which she runs together with her husband, who sells his records there.

248 HET DERDE SERVIES

Nieuwe Binnen-
weg 208-A
West ⑥
+31 (0)10 425 83 52
hetderdeservies.com

Hannie Mans sells porcelain, glass-and earthenware that roughly dates from 1900 to 1970 from all over the world. Expect typically Dutch Boerenbont sets of dishes next to Wedgwood and Limoges porcelain, Chinese tea sets and a large collection of intricately engraved crystal glasses.

249 DELFSHAVEN
MARITIEME KUNST-
EN ANTIEKHANDEL

Voorhaven 33
West ⑥
+31 (0)10 425 45 65
voc-rotterdam.com

Delve into Rotterdam's seafaring past and admire model ships, sextants, compasses, old maps and illustrations in this monumental building in historical Delfshaven. Besides maritime antiques they also sell 17th-and 18th-century Japanese and Chinese porcelain, silver and sculptures.

250 BERTUS ANTIEK
& CURIOSA

Nieuwe Binnen-
weg-83-B
Centre West ①
+31 (0)10 436 42 66
antiekencuriosa
bertus.nl

Looking for an original gift? Then drop in at Bertus and marvel at the little figurines, antique porcelain from China and Japan, silver and glassware, antique globes, Indonesian *wajang* dolls and lots of African masks. Bertus also has beautiful old furniture that will add character to your home. Lovingly collected and reasonably priced.

5 of the best
INTERIOR DESIGN SHOPS

---

251 METZ WONING-INRICHTING

Nieuwe Binnen-
weg 170
Centre West ①
+31 (0)10 436 45 66
metz-woning
inrichting.nl

Opened by Gerrit Metz in 1860, this furniture and design store has been in family hands for the past 160 years. With 3000 square metres of shopping space it is now the biggest interior design store in Rotterdam. They only sell 'real design'. Expect chairs and sofas by Gelderland, Leolux and Harvink, beds by Hülsta and lighting by Foscarini.

252 CONTEMPORARY SHOWROOM

Zaagmolenkade 41-42
North ⑥
+31 (0)6 422 734 80

Jarno Kooijman only sells vintage furniture in mint condition. If necessary, the sofas, chairs, tables and lamps are lovingly restored in his own professional workshop. These Italian, Dutch and Danish design items are really art works themselves.

253 VAN BINNEN

AT: DE GROENE PASSAGE
Mariniersweg 1
Centre East ②
+31 (0)10 240 93 79
vanbinnen.com

Van Binnen sells wonderful high-quality fabrics, bed linen, sustainably sourced wooden furniture, fabulous lamps and much, much more. Their whole collection is made 100% from natural materials. It's part of the Groene Passage, an eco-friendly and fairtrade shopping mall that also shows art works.

254 OUDSTIJL

Zwaanshals 494
North ③
+31 (0)6 174 639 38
oudstijl.nl

A Mecca for mid-century modern design, Oudstijl sells top pieces by famous Dutch design brands like Gispen and Pastoe, but you'll also find a lot of Danish design here and the occasional Italian item. The vintage pieces are carefully restored. It's fun to browse the shop, but items can also be bought online.

255 HARTMAN BINNEN-HUISADVISEURS

Mathenesserlaan 190
Centre West ①
+31 (0)10 436 15 43
hartmanbinnenhuis.nl

This interior design shop is fittingly located in a monumental building, designed by modernist architect Jo van den Broek. Hartman is a treasure trove filled with timeless design classics, both old and new. Think brands like Artifort, Vitra and Cassina, but also items made by young designers.

The 5 most stunning
PLANT SHOPS

256 STEK

Nieuwe Binnen-
weg 195-B
West ⑥
+31 (0)10 760 01 31
stekrotterdam.nl

The idea of five enthusiastic professionals who want to make the city greener and more sustainable. Stek is a mini gardening centre and an asylum for abandoned plants in one. Stek sells just about everything to make your garden or balcony a green paradise: from plants, seeds and gardening tools to books and birdhouses.

256 STEK

257 DANNY DE CACTUS

Schilderstraat 63-A
Centre West ①
+31 (0)6 132 138 87
dannydecactus.nl

With the right care, a cactus can be a friend for life. According to Danny, the trick is to lovingly neglect them. Visit his shop for all kinds of cacti, big and small, weirdly shaped succulents and agaves. Besides plants, Danny sells colourful home decoration items, jewellery and incense.

258 'T BOLLETJE

Lusthofstraat 76
Northeast ④
+31 (0)10 233 09 89
het-bolletje.nl

Known as 'that beautiful shop on the corner', 't Bolletje has been providing households in Kralingen and far beyond with the most beautiful bouquets for many years. Enjoy an espresso or cappuccino in this tastefully decorated shop while you're waiting for a fresh flower ensemble.

259 MK FLORAL DESIGN

Delistraat 34
South ⑤
+31 (0)10 484 99 05
mkfloraldesign.com

This enticing storefront leads into a veritable showroom for flowers. MK is Marit Kuypers, who lives and works in Katendrecht. She makes floral sculptures for special occasions, but you can also pop in for a bouquet, a beautiful vase, pot or bowl.

260 'S ZOMERS

Boekhorststraat 44-54
North ③
+31 (0)10 412 77 46
zomersbloemen.nl

You'll want to buy much more than fabulous bouquets or beautiful plants in this lush flower shop that's located inside the arch of a former railway viaduct. They also have an eclectic collection of elegant vases and furniture, perfumes and many other nice-to-have objects.

5 interesting
MODERN MAKERS
from Rotterdam

---

261 SUSAN BIJL

Mauritsweg 45-A
Centre West ①
+31 (0)10 751 07 79
susanbijl.nl

Susan Bijl's colourful nylon shopping bags are not only a local favourite, they have been spotted all over the world. For more than ten years this simple sturdy bag with the colourful slash design has made shoppers happy. The bag is lightweight, easy to fold, water repellent and absolutely tear proof. No need to ever use a plastic bag again.

262 MIRANDA VAN DER WAAL

Aelbrechtskolk 25-C
West ⑥
+31 (0)6 242 045 08
mirandavanderwaal.nl

Lamps, vases and even chandeliers: glass-blower Miranda van der Waal makes it all by herself. She uses old Venetian glass-blowing techniques, but gets her inspiration for shapes and decorations from Jugendstil and art deco designs. See her in action, or join a workshop, at her studio and shop in Delfshaven.

263 THE TALK OF THE TOWN

Keilestraat 5-A
West ⑥
+31 (0)6 188 320 58
ttottdesign.nl

Linda Post and her partner Leon Roozen have a knack for turning iconic pieces of Rotterdam into must-have items for your home. Think of a lamp made of Willemsbrug steel or a bench fabricated out of old Maastunnel escalator steps.

264 ZIGT JEWELRY

Nieuwe Binnen-
weg 107-A
Centre West ①
+31 (0)10 436 96 68
zigtsieraden.nl

There's a workshop at the back of this jewellery shop where the owners make their own rings, necklaces and bracelets. They use gold, silver and diamonds in combination with materials like silk and porcelain to make jewels that are modern and elegant, but with a classic twist.

265 OLGA KORSTANJE

Zaagmolenkade 40
North ③
+31 (0)6 287 857 61
olgakorstanje.com

There's a good chance you will find Olga Korstanje working on one of her bags in the back of her beautiful shop in the old North. She sells leather bags and accessories of her own brand O*, as well as a range of bags, scarfs and jewellery by other designers, selected for their craftsmanship and pure materials.

261 SUSAN BIJL

The 5 most
ORIGINAL SOUVENIRS
from Rotterdam

266 ROTTERZWAM GROWING KIT

rotterzwam.nl

Put your coffee grounds to good use with a RotterZwam growing kit *(zwam means mushroom)*. These black plastic tubs come with a batch of mycelium. Just add your own coffee grounds and some patience and you'll be eating home-grown oyster mushrooms in no time at all. The office at Bluecity and the plantation at Schiehaven aren't open to the public, but you'll find these growing kits in numerous shops around town.

267 DE ROTTERDAMSCHE OUDE

AT: CROMWIJK KAASDOK IN MARKTHAL

Ds. Jan Scharpstraat 298, Unit 48
Centre East ②
+31 (0)6 137 338 05
*derotterdamsche
oude.nl*

The idea for this old Gouda cheese was dreamt up in De Kuip football stadium, when a few businessmen and full-blooded Rotterdammers wanted their own old cheese (and not the one from Amsterdam!). De Rotterdamsche Oude is made by cheesemaker Dick Schumacher and is sold at Cromwijk Kaasdok inside Markthal, among other places.

268 PINEUT

AT: WAAR
Oude Binnenweg 116
Centre West ①
+31 (0)413 395 202
ditiswaar.nl

Pineut liqueur (*neut* is Dutch for a strong drink) is meant to be savoured. Buy a bottle filled with sustainably sourced herbs, spices, fruits or nuts, selected by the founders Femke van der Kuijp and Marlies van Iterson. Then add the alcohol (vodka or brandy) yourself. Depending on your choice, your DIY liqueur will be ready in two days to six weeks. You can find Pineut in various locations (see their website), for instance at WAAR.

269 NATTE T-DOEK

AT: TOURIST
INFORMATION OFFICE
Coolsingel 114
Centre East ②
+31 (0)10 790 01 85
rotterdam.info

The Rotterdam accent puts a lot of stress on the t's, also called a *natte t* ('wet t'). A dishcloth is called a *theedoek* in Dutch. So, here's your cloth to wipe away your wet t. The Natte T-doek is sold at various locations, for instance at the main tourist office.

270 ROTTERDAMSCHE CONFITUUR

Pretorialaan 6-A
South ⑤
+31 (0)6 145 562 77
rotterdamsche
confituur.nl

You can smell fresh fruit as it is being cooked for lovely organic jams like apple, lime and ginger or pineapple, banana and cranberry, as soon as you enter this small shop in Afrikaanderplein. It was founded to help local youngsters gain working experience. Have a thick slice of bread with jam and a cup of coffee, or buy a jar to take home.

DE HEF

40 BUILDINGS
TO ADMIRE

———

The 5 most impressive
HIGH RISES

271 TOREN OP ZUID

Wilhelminakade 123
South ⑤

The building occupied by telecom provider KPN was designed by the famous Italian architect Renzo Piano. Its eastern facade slants sideways and is held up by a 50-metre-tall steel column. Most striking though are the 900 lamps built into the facade, that can be individually controlled to project different images and colours.

272 DELFTSE POORT

Weena 505
Centre West ①

Known as the Nationale Nederlanden tower, these twin towers were built in 1992 after a design by Abe Bonnema. Standing at 151 metres, this used to be the highest building in the Netherlands. The building is partly open to the public, with a coffee corner on the ground floor and a food court, flexible work and meeting spaces, and a public gym on the second floor.

272 DELFTSE POORT

275 WORLD PORT CENTER & 273 MONTEVIDEO

273 MONTEVIDEO

Landverhuizersplein /
Otto Reuchlinweg
South ⑤

Since 2005, this massive skyscraper literally towers over its neighbours in Kop van Zuid. Its architect, Francine Houben, was inspired by New York high rises, as you can tell by the water tank. The giant M on top of the stacked building blocks can be interpreted as a reference to the building's name, Montevideo, or to Houben's architecture company, Mecanoo.

274 THE RED APPLE

Wijnbrugstraat
Centre East ②

This building with its striking red lines running down its facade houses apartments, offices and shops. It looks out over the old harbour. It was designed by KCAP Architects and commissioned by the Havensteder housing association. The name Red Apple alludes to New York (Rotterdam frequently being called Manhattan on the Maas River) and to the apple market that was located here around 1900.

275 WORLD PORT CENTER

Wilhelminakade 909
South ⑤
+31 (0)10 252 10 10
portofrotterdam.com

This was one of the first new view-defining buildings on the south bank of the river. World-renowned British architect Sir Norman Foster designed these headquarters for the port authority. The 124-metre-tall rounded building offers optimal views of the port, with a crow's nest on top.

5
GREAT ARCHITECTS
from Rotterdam

276 **ADRIAAN GEUZE**
(1960)
SCHOUWBURGPLEIN
Centre West ⓘ
west8.com

Landscape architect Adriaan Geuze is internationally renowned, with designs for the Jubilee Gardens in London and Governor's Island in New York. One of his first big projects was the redesign of Schouwburgplein in 1990. A majestic urban square according to some, but avoided by others because of its windswept, slippery surface. More unanimously lauded is his work around the new Central Station.

277 **EVERT AND HERMAN KRAAIJVANGER**
(1899-1978
AND 1903-1981)
HOLBEINHUIS
Coolsingel 65
Centre West ⓘ
holbeinhuis.nl

Brothers Evert and Herman Kraaijvanger played an important role in the post-war reconstruction of Rotterdam after World War II. They were responsible for dozens of striking modernist buildings in the city, including the Holbeinhuis office building, concert hall De Doelen (Schouwburgplein 50) and the shops of Vroom & Dreesmann and Peek & Cloppenburg in the Hoogstraat.

278 REM KOOLHAAS
(1944)
KUNSTHAL
Westzeedijk 341
Centre West ①
oma.com
kunsthal.nl

Rem Koolhaas is an internationally renowned architect. His Rotterdam based office OMA has designed buildings all over the world, including the CCTV building in Beijing and the Seattle Central Library. Rotterdam is also dotted with his bold, angular designs, the Rotterdam (2014), the Timmerhuis (2015) or the Kunsthal (1992) being the most notable examples. The Kunsthal heralded his international breakthrough.

280 PIET BLOM

279 HUGH MAASKANT

(1907-1977)
GROOTHANDELSGEBOUW
Stationsplein 45
Centre West ①
ghg.nl

Hugh Maaskant liked to refer to himself as 'the tallest architect'. Standing over two metres tall, he often was the tallest man in the room, but he also liked to design tall buildings. Take the Groothandelsgebouw (commerce building) for example, inspired by American architecture. Built in 1955, this is a monument of Rotterdam's reconstruction architecture. Maaskant also designed the Euromast, the Industriegebouw and the Hilton Hotel.

280 PIET BLOM

(1934-1999)
CUBE HOUSES
Overblaak 70
Centre East ②
+31 (0)10 414 22 85
kubuswoning.nl

Piet Blom was a member of the Dutch structuralism movement of the 1960s and 70s. One of his cube houses is now a small museum. He also rebuilt the nearby old harbour, a lively bar area which had been in ruins for years after the Second World War. From there you can also see Blom's remarkable high-rise called The Pencil at Kolk.

The 5 most interesting

HISTORIC BUILDINGS

281 VAN NELLE FACTORY

Van Nelleweg 1
West ⑥
+31 (0)10 750 40 00
*chabotmuseum.nl/
rondleiding-vannelle
fabriek*

This imposing industrial complex from 1931 is one of the icons of modernist architecture and was declared a UNESCO World Heritage site. It was designed by Brinkman and Van der Vlugt architects as an 'ideal factory': transparent to the outside world, with daylight providing pleasant working conditions. Guided tours are organised by the Chabot Museum in weekends.

282 VILLA VAN WANING

AT: NASSAUPARK
Nijverheidstraat 53
South ⑤
villavanwaning.nl

This former headquarters of cement brickworks Van Waning stood derelict for three decades, but has been restored to its former glory. Built in 1898, it was designed in art nouveau style and is now a monument. At the time of writing, a new restaurant has yet to open here.

283 THE WHITE HOUSE

Corner Wijnhaven /
Geldersekade
Centre East ②

Upon completion in the late 1890s, this 45-metre-high art nouveau tower block was the highest building in Europe. It was one of the few buildings in the city centre that survived the 1940 bombing. The patio of the grand cafe on the ground floor offers a great view of the old harbour.

284 WATER TOWER DE ESCH

Watertorenweg 180
Northeast ④

This water tower, built in the 1870s in neo-Roman and neo-Renaissance style with a Moorish dome, is the oldest remaining water tower in the country. It could hold up to a million litres of water. It was renovated in the 1970s and now holds apartments, offices and a very good cafe-restaurant on the ground floor.

285 CITY HALL

Coolsingel 40
+31 14 010
Centre East ②
rotterdam.nl/loket/
rondleiding-stadhuis

Next door to the post office and built in the same period, but in a more traditional neo-Renaissance style, after a design by Henri Evers. The symmetrical building surrounds an inner courtyard. Visitors (5 to 15 people) can take a free tour of the richly decorated city hall. The one-hour tour will take you past the council chamber, the wedding room, reception room and galleries. Reserve ahead.

5 of the most stunning
MODERN ICONS

---

286 TIMMERHUIS

Meent / Rodezand
Centre East ②

Look carefully, or you might just miss this mixed-use building by Rem Koolhaas' firm OMA. It was designed not to dominate the skyline, but to be absorbed by the city. This hovering cloud of steel and glass is connected to the old Timmerhuis, the headquarters for the post-war reconstruction of the city in the 1950s. Besides apartments, the building is also home to shops, restaurants and a public passage.

287 DEPOT BOIJMANS VAN BEUNINGEN

Museumpark 24
Centre West ①
+31 (0)10 441 94 00
boijmans.nl/depot

The story goes that a bowl of salad inspired MVRDV's Winy Maas for the design of the 40-metre-high, mirroring Depot (or 'flower pot', as locals call it). The vast collection of the Museum Boijmans Van Beuningen is stored inside. Buy a ticket – or even better: book a guided tour – to discover the building and see how artworks are stored and renovated.

290 **THE ROTTERDAM**

289 **SHIPPING AND TRANSPORT COLLEGE**

288 CENTRAL STATION

Stationsplein
Centre West ①
ns.nl

The best way to enter Rotterdam is through its Central Station. This wedge-shaped building, which is clad with stainless steel, is a collaboration between Benthem Crouwel Architects, MVSA Architects and West 8. The wooden ceiling, granite floors and large windows in the entranceway make for a pleasantly spacious building.

289 SHIPPING AND TRANSPORT COLLEGE

Lloydstraat 300
West ⑥
+31 (0)10 448 60 00
stc-group.nl

From this blue and white chequered building, the 2000 students of the Shipping and Transport College have a fabulous view of where they will work one day. The building by Neutelings Riedijk Architects with a 70-metre-high tower is shaped like a periscope.

290 THE ROTTERDAM

Wilhelminakade 177
South ⑤
derotterdam.nl

Standing 150 metres tall and over 100 metres wide, this is the largest building in the Netherlands and one of the largest in Europe. The irregular stacked building, representing a vertical city, was designed by OMA's Rem Koolhaas. Although initially criticised for adding more office space to a city that already has a problem with vacant office buildings, the Rotterdam has come to be revered for its 'in your face'-boldness.

The 5 most special

RELIGIOUS BUILDINGS

291 NORWEGIAN CHURCH

SJØMANNSKIRKEN
Westzeedijk 300
Centre West ①
+31 (0)10 436 51 23
sjomannskirken.no/
nederland

This wooden church was built in 1914 to draw sailors into the church and off the streets. It was a gift from Norway and was shipped as a 'do-it-yourself'-kit. Services are held in Norwegian, the church is open for visits except on Monday and Friday. It's also famous for its annual Christmas market.

292 PAULUS CHURCH

Mauritsweg 20
Centre West ①
+31 (0)10 411 81 32
pauluskerkrotterdam.nl

Conquer evil by doing good (Romans 12:21), that's the mission of this church. It became famous in the 1980s for helping the homeless, addicts, refugees and illegals. The copper building by British architect Will Alsop is new, but the mission and the church's open house policy have remained the same.

293 HILLEGONDA CHURCH

Kerkdreef 2
Hillegersberg
hillegondakerk.nl

This is the oldest church of Rotterdam, believed to have been built around 1500. The name is derived from a folk tale: a giantess called Hillegonda supposedly dumped an apron load of sand here, as depicted on this neighbourhood's (Hillegersberg) coat of arms.

294 ESSALAM MOSQUE

Vredesplein 7
South ⑤
+31 (0)10 419 36 66
essalamrotterdam.nl

The 50-metre-high minaret towers can be seen from afar. The Essalam mosque, the largest mosque in the Netherlands, was built between 2003 and 2010, after a design by architect Wilfred van Winden. The construction was delayed by financial problems and political opposition. Now, the mosque is a peaceful place of worship for 1500 men and women.

295 OLD CHURCH CHARLOIS

Charloisse
Kerksingel 35
South ⑤
+31 (0)6 155 448 90
oudekerkcharlois.nl

The first church to be built here dates from the 15th century, making the current building relatively 'new', the tower is now the oldest part (built in 1660). The tower's bells are still rung by hand. In 1868 the church was renovated and doubled in size. Don't forget to take a look at the impressive Hess organ.

294 ESSALAM MOSQUE

The 5 most characteristic
NEIGHBOURHOODS

296 TUIN VAN NOORD
(NORTH GARDEN)
Vrouwe Justitiahof
Noord ③

The former prison complex at Noordsingel, built in the 1860s, has recently opened its doors. Literally. The once hermetically sealed prison walls are now the gateway to a small public park, the cell blocks were turned into light and spacious family homes. The complex is truly a green and peaceful oasis around the corner from the always lively Zwart Janstraat.

297 WAGNERHOF
Vijverlaan 71
Northeast ④

Sugar trader Johan Dulfer bought Villa Nuova in 1904 and renamed it Villa Wagner after his favourite composer. He commissioned architect Jan van Teeffelen to build ten other villas, beautifully situated around a pond. The once colourful, but now mostly white Jugendstil villas with geometric details were all named after Wagner operas and characters.

298 JUSTUS VAN EFFENCOMPLEX

Justus van
Effenstraat
West ⑥

The Justus van Effencomplex is a social housing project from 1918 by architect Michiel Brinkman. The intimate yellow and red brick four-storey complex was built around inner courtyards, creating a village within the city. The building's central heating, the two elevators and the elevated gallery to reach the top apartments were very progressive for the time.

299 HOFJE VROUWE GROENEVELT'S LIEFDEGESTICHT

Vijverhofstraat 67
North ③
hofvrouwegroenevelt.nl

This inner courtyard for elderly and unmarried women had to move twice due to construction work. In 1902, the women settled into this location in Vijverhofstraat, near Hofbogen. The sixteen houses used to be basic one room with an attic. Showers were installed as late as 1992. Look for the mosaic with two angels around a clock, pointing down at two bats, messengers from the underworld.

300 THE PEPERKLIP

Rosestraat / Stootblok
South ⑤

This 500-metre-long apartment building in the shape of a paperclip is one of the most (in)famous housing projects of Rotterdam South. In 1982 the bold neo-rational design by architect Carel Weeber marked the end of small scale and 'narrow minded' building. The Peperklip had a bad image, but now tenants are proud again to live there.

5 of the most stunning
BRIDGES
you should cross

---

301 DE HEF

Prins Hendrikkade
to Nassaukade
South ⑤

A railway bridge connected the northern and southern parts of the city since the late 19th century. But in a harbour city like Rotterdam, something was due to go wrong. When a German steamship hit the bridge and heavily damaged it, the need for a vertical lift bridge became apparent. In 1927, the 70-metre-high De Hef was completed and immediately became an icon of the city.

302 ERASMUS BRIDGE

302 ERASMUS BRIDGE

Schiedamsedijk
to Posthumalaan
South ⑤

A bridge to connect the northern and southern parts of the city was part of the masterplan to revitalise the city's former harbour area on the south bank of the Nieuwe Maas River. The Erasmus Bridge, quickly nicknamed 'the Swan', was completed in 1996 and was followed by the rapid development of the Kop van Zuid (the head of south) quarter.

303 REGENTESSE BRIDGE

Posthoornstraat
to Glashaven
Centre East ②

It's difficult to imagine the grandiose surroundings of the old Wijnhaven, which was largely destroyed during World War II, but the copper lanterns and the stone lions on the corners of the Regentesse Bridge offer a glimpse of the past.

304 SPANJAARDS BRIDGE

Haringvliet
Centre East ②

A bridge has connected the Old Harbour district with Haringvliet harbour since the late 16th century. This monumental bridge was built in 1886, when all the bridges in the city were renovated. Spanjaards Bridge is a hydraulic bridge that uses drinking water to open and close.

305 RIJNHAVEN BRIDGE

Veerlaan to
Rijnhaven
noordzijde
South ⑤

Katendrecht, a former red light district, is quickly evolving into one of the trendiest places in town, filled with new bars, restaurants and cultural venues. The connection to Wilhelminapier that followed on the completion of the Rijnhaven Bridge only enhanced this development.

The 5 most inspirational

QUOTES ON BUILDINGS

306 'HEEL DE WERELD IS MIJN VADERLAND'
DESIDERIUS ERASMUS
AT: CENTRAL LIBRARY
ROTTERDAM
Hoogstraat 110
Centre East ②

Philosopher and humanist Desiderius Erasmus Roterodamus (1466-1536) lived in Rotterdam for only a few years, but apparently felt such a connection with the city that he added it to his name. References to Erasmus can be found all over Rotterdam. On the sidewall of the central library you find this quote: 'The whole world is my homeland.'

307 'WIE MEER WIL WETEN MOET WOORDEN ETEN'
GERRIT KOUWENAAR
Grote Visserij-
straat 120
West ⑥

Gerrit Kouwenaar (1923-2014) was a much lauded poet, author, journalist, resistance fighter and translator. He was also a contemporary of Lucebert and part of the Vijftigers literary movement, known for its spontaneous and experimental poetry. In later years his poems became more thoughtful. This line on the library wall says: 'Who wants to know more, must eat words.'

308 RIEN VROEGINDEWEIJ

Als iedereen ergens
anders vandaan komt
is niemand een vreemde

-Rien Vroegindeweij-

DE OMGEVING
VAN DE MENS
IS DE MEDEMENS

J.A. Deelder

309 JULES A. DEELDER

308 'ALS IEDEREEN ERGENS ANDERS VANDAAN KOMT IS NIEMAND EEN VREEMDE'
RIEN VROEGINDEWEIJ

West-Kruiskade /
Tiendplein
Centre West ①

'If everybody comes from somewhere else, nobody is a stranger', is a line by the poet Rien Vroegindeweij (1944) who captures the culture and people of Rotterdam in his articles, poems and plays. In 2006, he was given an Erasmus pin by the municipality, to honour his contributions to the city.

309 'DE OMGEVING VAN DE MENS IS DE MEDEMENS'
JULES A. DEELDER

Nieuwe Binnen-
weg 125
Centre West ①

Poet, performance artist and jazz lover Jules A. Deelder (1944-2019) was one of Rotterdam's most characteristic inhabitants. His straightforward and honest poems can be found in several places across the city. This one, written in blue neon, says 'The surroundings of man are his fellow men'. A little further on, at the crossing of Nieuwe Binnenweg and Mathenesserlaan, a life-size statue honours the former 'night mayor'.

310 'ALLES VAN WAARDE IS WEERLOOS'
LUCEBERT

AT: ROOF OF WILLEM
DE KOONING ACADEMY
Blaak 10
Centre East ②

These five words by Lucebert form one of the most cited poetry lines in the Netherlands. It means, 'Everything of worth is defenceless'. Lucebert (1924-1994) was an influential artist, connected to the Cobra movement as a painter, and to the literary movement the Vijftigers as a poet.

65 PLACES
TO DISCOVER
ROTTERDAM

The 5 most lovely
PARKS
to stroll around

---

311 VROESENPARK

Vroesenpad /
Vroesenlaan
North ③

This lovely park has a fish pond, playgrounds, tennis courts and grassy lawns. During summer, you'll see a lot of people on picnic blankets, putting skewers on the barbecue. No picnic blanket? Try the Vroesenpark pavillion, it has a lovely terrace and a fireplace inside.

313 ROOF PARK

312 ZUIDERPARK

Charlois
South ⑤

The biggest park in the city was built in the 1950s. A 2-kilometre-long hiking path winds its way through the trees, with plenty of fields, a playground and a beach. A great spot to start or end your exploration of the southern part of town.

313 ROOF PARK

Vierhavensstraat
(between
Marconiplein
and Hudsonplein)
West ⑥
dakparkrotterdam.nl

For decades, the Schiemond and Delfshaven neighbourhoods were separated by shops and other buildings. Now they are reconnected by the rooftop park that spans the car park on the shopping mall at Vierhavensstraat for over a kilometre. The park, 9 metres above street level, can be accessed from all streets. Or take the elevator from the shops.

314 PARK DE TWEE HEUVELS

Dwarsdijk 78
South ⑤

Two artificial hills give this park its name. They cover the remains of the old farms that had to make way for the expanding city. What looks like an old country estate is actually a park from the seventies. There are many different exotic trees to be found here, as well as kingfishers and bats.

315 THE PARK

Parkhaven 20
Centre West ①

This English landscape garden has meandering brooks, flowing fields of green and stately old trees. It was designed in 1852 by Jan David Zocher and his son, who subsequently also designed Amsterdam's Vondelpark.

The 5 most interesting places to
COMMEMORATE WWII

316 **FIRE BOUNDARY WALK**
TOURIST INFORMATION
Stationsplein 20
Centre West ①
Coolsingel 114
Centre East ②
+31 (0)10 790 01 85
brandgrens.nl

The German bombing on 14 May 1940 completely destroyed the historic city centre. To commemorate this dark episode in Rotterdam's history, the municipality traced a 12-kilometre tour along the periphery of the bombed area, the so-called Fire Boundary, marked by lighted, red signs in the pavement. Tourist information hands out free maps.

317 **LOODS 24**
Plein Loods 24
South ⑤
brandgrens.nl

Of the thousands of Jews who lived in Rotterdam before the war, only 852 were left in 1947. During the war, Jews were rounded up and brought to Loods 24, a silo in the port from where they were deported to concentration camps all over Europe. A monument to commemorate the city's Jewish history and the 686 children who were killed was placed at the location of the former silo.

317 **LOODS 24**

320 **ZADKINE'S 'THE DESTROYED CITY'**

318 MONUMENT FOR THE FORGOTTEN BOMBING

AT: PARK 1943
Rösener Manzstraat
West ⑥

Allied warplanes set course for the German war industry in Rotterdam's harbour on 31 May 1943. Due to bad weather, they hit Mathenesserweg, Schiedamseweg and Marconiplein in Rotterdam West instead, killing 300 to 400 civilians. In 1993 a monument was unveiled. The collapsed numbers refer to the date of this 'forgotten bombardment'.

319 THE OLD ZOO

Diergaardesingel
Centre West ①

Many animals of the old Rotterdam Zoo in Kruiskade died in the early days of the war. Supervisors opened the cages to save the surviving animals from the fires after the city was bombed. The result: ostriches walking along Coolsingel, two sea lions in Westersingel, chimpanzees hiding in a phone booth. The statue of a zebra in a pickle in a bird's nest (in Dutch: *Zebra in de Nesten*) was inaugurated in 2015.

320 ZADKINE'S 'THE DESTROYED CITY'

Plein 1940
Centre East ②

The Destroyed City by Ossip Zadkine, shows a crying man with his heart ripped out. It was created for the city and its inhabitants who lost their heart (the old city centre) in the bombardments. A yearly commemoration of the bombardments is held at the statue. It was gifted to the city by department store De Bijenkorf, which displays a miniature in its basement.

5 places to go to in the
HARBOUR

321 FUTURELAND

Europaweg 902
+31 (0)10 252 25 20
portofrotterdam.com/
nl/eropuit/futureland

Imagine building a port 10 kilometres out to sea out of nothing. In the FutureLand visitor centre you can learn about this amazing engineering feat and get a real sense of the scale of Europe's biggest harbour. From FutureLand, you can take a boat or a bus excursion to explore the port. You can get to FutureLand by car or by fast ferry from Hoek van Holland.

322 PENINSULA ROZENBURG

In the heart of the ports lies a green oasis, a man-made peninsula that has become a wildlife refuge. Walk past ponds, reeds and dunes, see grazing Highland cows and Konik horses, and admire the many birds and butterflies that flock here. At the entrance there is an information centre. Reach the peninsula by car (A15 direction Europoort) or with the fast ferry from Hoek van Holland.

323 MAASVLAKTE 2 BEACH

Maasvlakte

This latest extension of the port includes the biggest beach in Rotterdam. It's popular year-round for water sports, kites and long walks (dogs are allowed). Have a snack at snackbar Smickel Inn and marvel at the cargo ships entering the harbour that pass right in front of you. We recommend going by car.

324 HET KERINGHUIS

Maeslantkering-
weg 139
Hoek van Holland
+31 (0)88 797 06 30
keringhuis.nl

The Maeslantkering is a storm surge barrier. The two floating gates close when needed, in case of storm and high water, to prevent flooding. It's part of the Delta Works and one of the biggest moving structures on earth. In the Keringhuis information centre you can learn more about this amazing engineering feat and how the Dutch cope with living beneath sea level.

325 WORLD HARBOUR DAYS

+31 (0)10 252 49 49
wereldhavendagen.nl

During the first weekend of September, Rotterdam's port opens to the public. Visitors get the chance to experience the working harbour up close, take a look behind the scenes of the biggest port companies, climb on board the deck of a marine ship, watch boat races and enjoy a laser and fireworks show.

The 5 best
BOAT VISITS

326 SS ROTTERDAM

3e Katendrechtse-
hoofd 25
South ⑤
+31 (0)10 297 30 90
ssrotterdam.nl

A former flagship of the Holland America Line, the ss Rotterdam was launched by queen Juliana in 1959. Now it's permanently moored in the docks. Get a tour from a former employee, enjoy a cocktail in the captain's lounge, dine while looking out over the city's skyline, and stay in one of the 254 hotel rooms, in the original fifties style.

327 THE SHIPS OF THE MARITIME MUSEUM

Leuvehaven 1
Centre East ②
+31 (0)10 413 26 80
maritiemmuseum.nl/en

With a ticket to the Maritime Museum you can also visit their collection of 19th-and 20th-century boats. They are well maintained, fully functioning ships and in the summer months, they'll even take you on a tour.

328 DE BUFFEL

Koningskade 2
Hellevoetsluis
+31 (0)6 124 458 15
debuffel.nl

This armoured cruiser, a war ship, was built in Scotland after 1850. It was quickly turned into an accommodation ship, and later a museum ship. Visit the ship and walk through its 145 years of history. It's fun for kids especially, with interactive games and a play deck.

326 SS ROTTERDAM

329 SPIDO HARBOUR TOUR

Willemsplein 85
Centre West ①
+31 (0)10 275 99 99
spido.nl

The Spido tourist vessels leave from the base of the Erasmus Bridge and will show you spectacular views of the bridge, the Rotterdam skyline, the old harbour places and the working port. In summer, there are different options, like an extended harbour tour including the most recent additions to the harbour and a summer evening tour.

330 DE PANNENKOEKEN-BOOT

Parkhaven 13
West ⑥
+31 (0)10 436 72 95
rotterdam.pannen-
koekenboot.nl

Everyone loves Dutch pancakes (*pannenkoeken*): they're bigger than the American variety and heavier than French *crêpes*. They can be eaten with sweet toppings like syrup, or with savoury ones like cheese or bacon. The pancake boat takes you on a 75-minute boat trip and serves pancakes on the way – as many as you like.

The 5 most
QUIET PLACES
in town

---

331 HISTORIC GARDEN SCHOONOORD

Kievietslaan 8
Centre West ①
tuinschoonoord.nl

This historical 1,2-hectare garden was designed by J.D. Zocher in English landscape style. The garden is home to some special trees and over 1000 plants. There are koi carp in the pond and a tawny owl has been spotted here.

332 CASTLE RUINS HUIS TEN BERGHE

AT: CEMETERY OF
HILLEGONDA CHURCH
Kerkstraat 43
North ③
hillegondakerk.nl

The cemetery of the Hillegonda church, the oldest in the city, in northern Hillegersberg holds quite a secret: there are castle ruins located in the cemetery. This 13th-century castle Huis ten Berghe was destroyed during the Hook and Cod wars, a power struggle within the elite of the County of Holland that took place in the 14th and 15th century.

333 TROMPENBURG TUINEN & ARBORETUM

Honingerdijk 86
Northeast ④
+31 (0)10 233 01 66
trompenburg.nl

Trompenburg is a beautiful collection of botanical gardens with different atmospheres. It's a good place to get away from the hustle and bustle of city life and to admire the trees (many species of oak, beech and holly), flowering plants and cacti. It boasts a teahouse, an aviary, a shop and a restaurant as well.

334 SLOTVIJVER KRALINGEN

Slotbrug 1
Northeast ④

Once upon a time there was a castle here named Slot Honingen. Its ruins were demolished in 1672, but the pond is the remainder of its moat and is surrounded by centuries-old trees and stately mansions, including Het Oude Slot (the old castle), which dates from 1870. You'll find the house at Slotlaan 29. In the stained glass window you can see the old Honingen castle.

335 CROOSWIJK CEMETERY

Kerkhoflaan 1
Northeast ④

This oldest municipal cemetery was founded in 1832. It's partly laid out in classic English garden style, which makes for a peaceful and green environment. There are more than 17.000 graves here, with special Roman-Catholic and Islamic sections. There are also more than a 1000 graves of people who perished in the 1940 bombing of the city.

331 HISTORIC GARDEN SCHOONOORD

5 of the most interesting
STATUES

336 DESIDERIUS ERASMUS

Grotekerkplein
Centre East ②

Humanist, philosopher and theologian Desiderius Erasmus was born in Rotterdam around 1466. The influence of his works like *The Praise of Holly* and *The Ecclesiastes* reached far and wide. This statue was erected in 1622, making it the oldest statue in the Netherlands.

337 DIJKWERKERS

Maashaven Oostzijde
South ⑤

The two *Dijkwerkers* (dike workers) carry a heavy load of basalt to build a dike. This monument was made by artist Ek van Zanten and symbolises the struggle against the water, and the solidarity and cooperation that entails. You'll find it on the shore at the junction of Maashaven and Paul Krugerstraat.

338 FIKKIE

Oude Binnenweg 122
Centre West ①

The local student fraternity donated Fikkie the dog to the city in 1963. The bronze terrier became a popular gathering point for young protesters *(provos)* in the 1960s. It was stolen several times, retrieved, and moved to its current location. The turd was a gift from the municipal garbage collectors and was added later.

339 THE GIANT OF ROTTERDAM

AT: WIJKPARK
OUDE WESTEN
West-Kruiskade 11
Centre West ⓘ

Rigardus Rijnhout (1922-1959) was nicknamed 'the giant of Rotterdam' because of his impressive height (2,37 metres). 'You often met with scorn and were taunted but you didn't hate people for it, because you had a heart of gold', his father said at the funeral upon Rigardus' death at the age of 36. A life-size statue (including his shoes) was erected in 2011, near where he lived.

340 THE GUARD

AT: SKATEPARK
WESTBLAAK
Opposite
Westblaak 147
Centre West ⓘ

Local skaters organised a petition to have this statue erected in their skatepark at Westblaak. It shows a robot that stands guard at the top of a 3-metre-high comet shard. Artist Hans van Bentem was inspired by the Japanese anime series Gundam when creating this ceramic statue.

340 THE GUARD

The 5 must-visit places in
HISTORICAL DELFSHAVEN

---

341 OLD OR PILGRIMS FATHERS CHURCH

Aelbrechtskolk 20
West ⑥
+31 (0)10 477 41 56
pelgrimvaderskerk.nl

The 'pilgrim fathers' were Calvinists who fled England in the early 17th century and moved to the Low Countries before setting sail for the New World and founding America. They started their journey in Delfshaven at the little harbour adjacent to the early 15th-century reformed church that now bears their name. It remains a mystery whether the pilgrims actually visited this church. (Open on Friday and Saturday afternoons.)

342 PIET HEYN'S BIRTHPLACE

Piet Heynstraat 6
West ⑥

Admiral Piet Heyn became a national hero after looting the Spanish silver from a ship that was anchored at Cuba, in 1628. The treasure he brought back home was worth the equivalent of half a billion euros. His house of birth in Delfshaven was demolished, but rebuilt in the 19th century as a tribute. His statue is around the corner, in Piet Heynplein.

343 EETHUISJE VAN DELFSHAVEN

Mathenesser-
dijk 436-A
West ⑥
+31 (0)10 425 49 17

What better way to end a visit to Delfshaven than with a meal in this old-fashioned *gezellige* (cosy) eatery? The menu features typical Dutch fare – meat, potatoes and veg – and changes daily. Food like your mother would make, if she were Dutch. The atmosphere in this family-run restaurant is very friendly, and so are the prices.

344 WINDMILL DISTILLEERKETEL

Voorhaven 210
West ⑥
+31 (0)10 477 91 81

Of the five windmills on the Delfshaven skyline, only one survived. Built in the early 18th century, it was used to produce malt for the *jenever* (gin) industry. In 1899 the mill burned down, and again in 1940. But it was renovated twice and is now used to grind grain for local bakeries.

345 CAFÉ DE OUDE SLUIS

Havenstraat 7
West ⑥
+31 (0)10 477 30 68
cafedeoudesluis.nl

This brown pub opened in the early 20th century and hasn't changed much since. The walls are large reliefs made by Italian terrazzo workers, who specialised in the construction of tile floors. The old, wooden lock-to which the bar's name refers-is located behind the pub and dates from around 1400.

The 5 best places to
DISCOVER THE SOUTH

---

346 AFRIKAANDERPLEIN
South ⑤

Cross Erasmus Bridge and head straight to Pretorialaan. Here you'll find a combination of new coffee bars, hip eateries, galleries and old speciality shops. There's a large, multicultural fresh market in Afrikaanderplein on Wednesdays and Saturdays. You'll also find a nice park, a botanical garden and one of the best ice-cream places in town (IJssalon Nino) here.

347 VERHALENHUIS BELVÉDÈRE
Rechthuislaan 1
South ⑤
+31 (0)10 720 09 97
verhalenhuis
rotterdam.nl

This corner building on Katendrecht has a fascinating history: it's been a restaurant, a jazz bar, a wrestling venue and an artist's home. It now hosts regular exhibitions and recitals, sharing stories about local residents and their art, and serves communal meals. In the attic, the home of artists Wally Elenbaas and his wife Esther Hartog have been restored.

348 KIEFHOEK

Hendrik Idoplein 2
South ⑤
urbanguides.nl/en/
tours/the-kiefhoek

The red doors, yellow window frames and blue gates were inspired by De Stijl. The efficiently built houses (61 square metres) could fit a family of six. The entire neighbourhood was renovated in the nineties, but one house has been preserved as it was in 1930. Visit this museum on appointment.

349 OLD CHARLOIS

South ⑤

The historic part of Charlois dates back to the 15th century. You can almost feel the history around the Charloisse Kerksingel. Visit the church and walk past the speciality shops in Gouwstraat. Then walk up Boergoensevliet towards Kromme Zandweg, next to Zuiderpark. Here you'll find an old country estate (De Oliphant), a windmill that's open on Saturday afternoons and a lovely brasserie (Koriander) with a large sunny terrace.

350 HEIJPLAAT

South ⑤
heijplaat.com

Heijplaat is a lovely garden city built between the shipbuilding and repair docks of the Rotterdamse Droogdok Maatschappij (RDM). Three churches dominate the central axis. When the dry docks closed in the eighties, the houses became popular with artists. There are schools for architects and vocational education. To get there, take the Watertaxi from Marconistraat.

5 *interesting*
PUBLIC TRANSPORT ROUTES

---

351 **WATERTAXI**
+31 (0)10 403 03 03
watertaxirotterdam.nl

The Watertaxi is a fast way to travel between 50 landing stages in and around Rotterdam. Book a seat on the taxi online or by phone. In addition, there are some shuttle services, for instance between M4H/Marconistraat and Heijplaat. Check the website.

354 **MAASTUNNEL**

352 TRAM LINE 4

ret.nl

This 10-kilometre line runs from leafy and family-friendly Hillegersberg in the East through the trendy Oude Noorden quarter and the city centre to the intersection of Delfshaven and Spangen in the West.

353 METRO TO HOEK VAN HOLLAND

ret.nl

Visit the beach by public transport: metro line B takes you right from the heart of Rotterdam to the beach at Hoek van Holland in about half an hour. On the way, it stops at Schiedam, Vlaardingen and Maassluis. In Hoek van Holland, you can enjoy the beach or a long walk across the dunes. End your day in one of the cosy local eateries.

354 MAASTUNNEL

Parkkade 30 /
Charloisse Hoofd 25
South / West ⑤⑥

Take one of the 17-metre-long wooden escalators and walk underneath the Maas River in a tunnel that opened in 1942. Located between 's-Gravendijkwal (close to the Euromast) and Doklaan, the tunnel connects the northern and southern parts of the city. It's especially fun to take your bike on the escalators.

355 WATERBUS

waterbus.nl

Rotterdam was built around the river, so what better way to travel than across the water? The Waterbus runs twice every hour between Dordrecht in the east and Rotterdam, Erasmus Bridge. You can also visit the mills at Kinderdijk by Waterbus.

5 places to discover
HOEK VAN HOLLAND

356 WALKING THROUGH THE DUNES

Hoek van Holland

Although Hoek van Holland is about 35 kilometres away from Rotterdam, the connection via metro line B makes this seaside resort (which is part of the municipality of Rotterdam) seem a lot closer. From the metro stop, you can walk straight into the dunes. The hustle and bustle of the city suddenly seems far away.

357 PELE SURF SHACK

AT: THE 'SPORTS BEACH'
Rechtestraat 24
Hoek van Holland
pelesurfshack.nl

Enjoy a laidback surf atmosphere on a quiet part of the beach, delicious vegan dishes and a view of the sunset: Pele Surf Shack is the natural ending to a relaxing day at the beach. The shack is located on what is locally known as 'the sports beach' and is sandwiched in between two surf schools.

358 FRIES FROM A BUNKER

AT: SNACKBAR DE PIER
Koningin Emma-
boulevard 11
Hoek van Holland
+31 (0)174 384 797
snackbardepier.nl

As the gateway to the port of Rotterdam, Hoek van Holland was of great strategic importance during World War II. Hundreds of bunkers were built here, some of which have been repurposed in an interesting way. Like Snackbar de Pier, which was built against a former German bunker. They bake delicious *'raspatat'* (fries made of potato dough). Order some to go and enjoy them while you walk along the nearby pier.

359 PLSTK CAFÉ

AT: DE ZEETOREN
Helmweg 7
Hoek van Holland
+31 (0)174 785 016
plstkcafe.nl

Located in the middle of the dunes, with no buildings in sight: you won't find a better terrace than PLSTK's in Hoek van Holland, or anywhere else in Rotterdam. This pleasant bar-restaurant is located in the Zeetoren (sea tower), which was the site of a radar installation during World War II.

360 FERRY TO MAASVLAKTE 2

Berghaven /
Futureland
Hoek van Holland
hoeksveer.nl

Sunbathing on the beach at Hoek van Holland can feel slightly strange, with the port and its heavy industry and container terminals in the background. But why not check it out from up close? Between 1 April and 1 October, a ferry rides from Berghaven in Hoek van Holland to Futureland, the harbour information centre at Maasvlakte 2. On the way, you pass the world's biggest cargo ships and sunbathing seals.

5 of the most
FAMOUS
ROTTERDAMMERS

---

361 JULES A. DEELDER

Corner of Nieuwe
Binnenweg /
Mathenesserlaan
Centre West ①

Rotterdam's 'night mayor' Jules A. Deelder (1944-2019) was a famous Dutch poet, known jazz connoisseur, style icon (always wearing bespoke black suits) and a prominent supporter of Rotterdam West's football club Sparta. His poem *To Ari,* written for his daughter, is printed on the 900-metre-long wall of the Benelux Tunnel, which starts west of Schiedam. There's a statue honouring Deelder at the corner of Nieuwe Binnenweg and Mathenesserlaan, in front of cafe Ari.

362 MARLIES DEKKERS

Witte de Withstraat 2
Centre East ②
+31 (0)6 152 767 33
marliesdekkers.com

Her lingerie is sold worldwide, but Marlies Dekkers (1964) always returns to Rotterdam, where she has been living for years. Dekkers uses trends in urban subcultures she encounters here as inspiration for her designs. Her first shop in the Netherlands opened in Witte de Withstraat in 2004.

363 ROBIN VAN PERSIE

STADIUM WOUDESTEIN
Honingerdijk 110
Northeast ④
excelsiorrotterdam.nl

Before his transfer to Feyenoord at the age of 12, Robin van Persie (1983) trained at football club Excelsior in Kralingen (he went on to play for Arsenal and Manchester United). Young Van Persie grew up on Jaffadwarsstraat and sometimes walked the entire 2,5 kilometres to his club's stadium while kicking a ball. The stadium opened its Robin van Persie stand in 2010.

364 NEELIE KROES

As a European Commissioner for competition, liberal politician Neelie Kroes (1941) imposed huge fines on Google, Microsoft, large banks and other multinationals that had exploited their monopoly positions or had formed cartels. Kroes was born in Nieuw-Mathenesse, close to Schiedam, and was a member of the municipal government in the 1970s.

365 PIM FORTUYN

Pim Fortuynplaats
Centre East ②

The murder of Pim Fortuyn (1948-2002), a likely candidate to become the next Dutch prime minister, left the country in a shock. Fortuyn was a populist politician with strong views, but nobody could have foreseen a political murder. Fortuyn was born in a village near Amsterdam, but enjoyed initial success in Rotterdam: initially as a professor in sociology, later as a local politician. A statue was erected in Pim Fortuynplaats square.

5 things you probably didn't know
ABOUT ROTTERDAM

366 GREEN CITY

Rotterdam is known for its bold architecture and its world-class port, but is actually a very green city as well. There are more than 600.000 trees, making it the city with the most trees per capita in the Netherlands. There are a few really old ones, like a late-19th-century plane tree that received its own little island at Westersingel and a sycamore (1851) on Lijnbaan that survived the bombing of the city.

367 THE 10TH CAPE VERDEAN ISLAND

Heemraadsplein
West ⑥

Rotterdam has the largest community of Cape Verdeans (± 15.000) in the Netherlands and is therefore called 'the 10th Cape Verdean island'. Three quarters of the Cape Verdean population live in Delfshaven. Heemraadsplein square is a popular meeting place and the site of the yearly Festa de São João do Porto. Look for the street sign that says *Pracinha de Quebrod* (square of the poor souls).

368 LIJNBAAN

Lijnbaan /
Korte Lijnbaan
Centre West ①

A car free shopping promenade was a novelty in 1953, in fact Lijnbaan was the first in the world. It was designed by Van den Broek & Bakema architects and is considered a highlight of the reconstruction era. Three quarters of a century later, it's still a popular place to spend money, though nowadays mostly in international chain stores.

369 THE LARGEST PORT IN EUROPE

portofrotterdam.nl

The Port of Rotterdam is the largest in Europe, and it holds its own in between nine Asian cities in the world's top ten. Some staggering figures: the port covers 12.500 hectares and has a total length of over 40 kilometres. About 30.000 ocean-going vessels and 100.000 river barges anchor here every year. The annual throughput is 470 million tonnes.

370 ROTTERDAM COULD HAVE BEEN A CLASSICAL CITY

Right after the bombing of 14 May 1940 city architect W.G. Witteveen made a plan to clean up and rebuild the city. According to its critics, the plan focussed too much on repairing and restoring perimeter blocks and monumental facades, and not enough on innovation. In 1944 Witteveen resigned, paving the way for a more modernist city.

5 striking examples of
DIY ROTTERDAM

---

371 KLUSWONINGEN
(DIY HOUSES)
Pompstraat 44
South ⑤

Derelict houses are sold for a low price and then completely renovated and restyled by the new inhabitants. This current trend of DIY houses actually started in Rotterdam. It's a way to create attractive housing in deprived urban areas. It started in the Wallisblock in Spangen (Rotterdam West) in 2004 but has since become popular all over the city. A fine example is the 'black pearl' in Charlois, at Pompstraat 44.

372 OASE
Schiehaven 15-A
West ⑥
oaserotterdam.nl

Visit a vintage market, trade your plant cuttings, visit a lecture or attend an early morning mindfulness session. Oase isn't just an ecological hub, the founders say, but also a cultural, social and healthy one. The goal, however, is clear and straightforward: it's a meeting spot made for *Rotterdammers*, by *Rotterdammers*.

373 OPZOOMEREN

Schiedamsedijk 55-A
Centre West ①
+31 (0)10 213 10 55
opzoomermee.nl

It started at the end of the eighties with a set of brooms for sweeping and a set of geraniums to cheer up Opzoomerstraat in Delfshaven. *Opzoomeren* has since then become an official verb: it means to take initiative to clean up shared public space. It's a way for occupants to collectively take control of their streets and liven up their neighbourhood and is immensely popular in Rotterdam.

374 BLUECITY
TROPICANA

Maasboulevard 100
Centre East ②
+31 (0)10 307 22 47
bluecity.nl

This former tropical swim paradise was derelict before a group of entrepreneurs known as BlueCity decided to turn the fate of this remarkable building around. Now, it's the site of businesses such as RotterZwam, which grows oyster mushrooms from coffee grounds, and the Aloha cafe-restaurant, which roasts its own coffee. The building's philosophy is to reuse and recycle and to create a circular economy.

375 URBAN FARMING
AT: ROTTERDAMSE MUNT

Rosestraat 200
South ⑤
+31 (0)6 386 901 64
rotterdamsemunt.nl

Rotterdam is a front runner in urban agriculture. Well-known examples are 'De Voedseltuin' (Keileweg 5) and 'Dakakker' (on a roof at Schiekade 189), but there are many more vegetable patches to be found around the city. Visit 'Rotterdamse Munt', a community herb garden or 'De Pluktuin' (a fruit picking garden) at RFC-weg 190.

SONNEVELD HOUSE

55 PLACES
TO ENJOY CULTURE

———

5

MUSEUMS
YOU SHOULDN'T MISS

---

376 NEDERLANDS FOTOMUSEUM
Statendam 1
South ⑤
+31 (0)10 203 04 05
nederlands fotomuseum.nl

The Dutch photo museum owns a large collection of works by contemporary photographers and the archives of photographers such as Ed van der Elsken and Cas Oorthuys. Temporary exhibitions at the museum focus on documentary, experimental photography, by photographers from the past and the present, or new talent.

377 KUNSTHAL
AT: MUSEUMPARK
Westzeedijk 341
Centre West ①
+31 (0)10 440 03 01
kunsthal.nl

Architect Rem Koolhaas designed this exhibition venue on the south side of Museumpark. This 'art hall' doesn't have a collection of its own, but curates over 20 high profile, annual exhibitions in genres such as modern art, fashion, photography and design. Don't forget to stop at the museum shop, where the offer changes regularly to match the many exhibitions.

378 WERELDMUSEUM

Willemskade 25
Centre West ①
+31 (0)10 270 71 72
wereldmuseum.nl

The local yacht club used to have its home base here. Gifts were brought in from all over the world. The collection kept on growing after the municipality bought the building in 1885 and turned it into a museum. The vast collection of utensils, religious objects and weapons among others illustrates the close historical connection between this port city and the rest of the world.

379 HET NATUUR-HISTORISCH MUSEUM ROTTERDAM

AT: MUSEUMPARK
Westzeedijk 345
Centre West ①
+31 (0)10 436 42 22
hetnatuurhistorisch.nl

Besides stuffed animals, fossils and huge skeletons, the Natural History Museum has a humoristic collection of 'dead animals with a story', like a seagull that crashed into a trauma helicopter and a hedgehog with its head stuck in a McFlurry cup. Look out for the show-offs: the animals with the longest neck, biggest mouth, greatest appetite or hottest fart!

380 STEDELIJK MUSEUM SCHIEDAM

Hoogstraat 112
Schiedam
+31 (0)10 246 36 66
stedelijkmuseum schiedam.nl

Schiedam isn't exactly Rotterdam, but it's part of the city's public transportation network and therefore easy to reach. The Stedelijk Museum Schiedam has a good collection of Dutch post-war art, including many works by Cobra painters such as Karel Appel, Constant and Corneille. To get there, take tramline 21 or 24 from the city's Central Station and get off at Schiedam, Koemarkt.

5 places to enjoy
STREET CULTURE

381 **ANNIE M.G. SCHMIDTPLEIN**
South ⑤

Nestled in between the new Theater Zuidplein, the biggest swimming pool of Rotterdam, the public library, a shopping centre and bus and metro station Zuidplein, the Annie M.G. Schmidtplein always draws a crowd. Artwork *The Splash* (an 'open-air swimming pool') is the perfect place for people-watching.

382 **WEST-KRUISKADE**
Centre West ①

The West-Kruiskade was and still is a popular place to shop for exotic wares, to grab a bite to eat, and most of all to see and be seen. Especially on Friday nights, cars cruise up and down trying to attract the gaze of passers-by. Settle down on a terrace and enjoy the show.

383 GROTEKERKPLEIN
Centre East ②

One of the few pleasant green and quiet spots in the city centre, Grotekerkplein draws a mostly young crowd in the evenings and shopping families during the day. An open-air theatre by Atelier Kempe Thill provides cover for performances and acts as a picture frame for the square.

384 MAASBOULEVARD
South ⑤

Besides offering spectacular views of the river, the bridges and the skyline of Rotterdam, Maasboulevard is a popular spot for working out, cycling and jogging or just lounging in the sun. If you want to soak up the energy of a vibrant waterfront, this is the place to go.

385 ZWART JANSTRAAT
North ③

The busiest shopping street of the Old North is a multicultural gathering place that brings together both Moroccan grocers and fast food places, old brown bars and a gem of a karaoke place, Tropica. The 'Zwart Jan' caters to everyone's fancy, and thanks to recent interventions it is becoming a more attractive place for a leisurely stroll.

The 5 most innovative places to see
CONTEMPORARY ART

386 **GARAGE ROTTERDAM**
Goudsewagen-
straat 27
Centre East ②
+31 (0)10 737 08 75
garagerotterdam.nl

The curators of this exhibition space in a former garage focus on the latest developments in contemporary art – high quality but not too high brow. Garage Rotterdam cooperates with Museum Boijmans Van Beuningen and combines its thematic group expositions with lectures and debates, concerts and culinary events. Young makers get to pitch their ideas on Wednesday nights.

387 **KUNSTINSTITUUT MELLY**
Witte de With-
straat 50
Centre West ①
+31 (0)10 411 01 44
kunstinstituutmelly.nl

Kunstinstituut Melly is not afraid of experimenting. It cooperates with artists, thinkers and writers to tackle current topics in temporary exhibitions. It has been a forerunner on the international arts scene since 1990 and has launched the careers of curators, critics and researchers.

386 **GARAGE ROTTERDAM**

388 TENT

**Witte de With-
straat 50**
Centre East ②
+31 (0)10 201 09 60
tentrotterdam.nl

TENT is located in the same building as the Kunstinstituut Melly, but is a separate organisation that focuses on current art from and about Rotterdam within an international context.

389 A TALE OF A TUB

**Justus van Effen-
straat 44**
West ⑥
a-tub.org

Four young female curators started this gallery in the former bathhouse of the beautiful Justus van Effencomplex. A Tale of a Tub sets out to explore the boundaries of the art world, looking for new ways of presentation and interaction with the public. Think exhibitions of exciting (and prize-winning) young artists, regular performances, film screenings and artist talks.

390 BRUTUS

Keileweg 10-18
West ⑥
brutus.nl

Brutus is the brainchild of Atelier Van Lieshout and aims to be an 'artist-driven playground'. It is a 6000-square-metre experimental zone for cutting-edge culture that will be part of the bigger transformation of the M4H area where artists become a permanent fixture.

The 5 most special
MUSEUMS

---

391 MUSEUM HOUSE OUDE NOORDEN

Jacob Catsstraat 23
North ③
+31 (0)6 429 234 58
museumwoning.nl

Travel back in time and see what it was like to live in Rotterdam in the early 20th century when people still slept in a cupboard bed and kept a canary to warn them about carbon dioxide poisoning by the coal stove. A second house transports you into the bright and optimistic fifties and sixties. Visit on Wednesday afternoons or make an appointment. The entrance is free and the guided tour is really interesting.

392 DUTCH PINBALL MUSEUM

Voorhaven 12
West ⑥
+31 (0)6 214 64 697
dutchpinball
museum.com

The purchase of one pinball machine soon led to another, and another and another. Now, the pinball museum fills a warehouse with over 60 pinball machines, from rare antiques to modern ones and even one designed by the owner. Open on weekends and Wednesday afternoons.

393 TAX AND CUSTOMS MUSEUM

Parklaan 14-16
Centre West ①
+31 (0)88 151 49 00
bdmuseum.nl

You're never too old to learn about taxes. This museum will show you everything there is to know about this not so fun albeit essential part of our life. The museum has a surprisingly extensive collection, from uniforms and costumes, to measuring instruments, smuggle ware, silver, glass and a modern art collection. Children can be customs officers and learn about smuggling.

394 SONNEVELD HOUSE

Jongkindstraat 12
Centre West ①
+31 (0)10 440 12 00
huissonneveld.nl

This villa near Rotterdam's Museumpark is one of the best-preserved homes built in the Dutch Functionalist style. It was designed for the Sonneveld family in the 1930s by Brinkman and Van der Vlugt, of the Van Nelle Factory and Feyenoord Stadium. The house is filled with Gispen furniture and shows how a prominent Rotterdam family lived in the modernist age.

395 MUSEUM FOR DISCARDED STATUES

Kleinpolderplein
West ⑥

Underneath the biggest traffic intersection of Rotterdam, you'll find a growing collection of discarded statues *(museum voor verweesde beelden)* that either had to be moved or became unwanted. Integrating art here is an attempt to slowly transform a car-dominated area into a more diverse and attractive space.

The 5 best galleries to
BUY ART

---

396 GALLERY UNTITLED

**Koningsvelde-
straat 14
North ③
+31 (0)6 514 267 58
galleryuntitled.nl**

Gallery Untitled is located in an old schoolhouse, spanning over 350 square metres. It was founded by photographer and art director Lenny Oosterwijk. Aside from exciting exhibitions by artists like Carlijn Kingma, Pallotti and Ulrike Främbs, they also regularly host events, such as concerts and lectures. Open from Friday through Sunday, or by appointment. Don't forget to visit the adjacent restaurant, named 'de Kok en de Tuinman'.

397 FRANK TAAL GALERIE

**Van Speykstraat 129
Centre West ①
+31 (0)6 414 009 27
franktaal.nl**

Owners Frank Taal and Hans Franke distinguish themselves by actively promoting art, with 8 to 10 exhibitions a year. They show sculptures, photography, drawings and paintings, and also organise events outside their white walls.

398 ZERP GALERIE

Van Oldenbarnevelt-
straat 120-A
Centre West ①
+31 (0)10 846 37 30
zerp.nl

After working as a painter and a gallery manager in Amsterdam for years, Zic Zerp established his own gallery for contemporary art in 2011. Zerp wants to foster the interaction between established and upcoming artists, and between those working in different genres like painting, drawing, photography, and video and sculpture art.

399 GALERIE ATELIER HERENPLAATS

Schietbaanstraat 1
Centre West ①
+31 (0)10 214 11 08
herenplaats.nl

Since 1991, Atelier Herenplaats offers artists with a mental disability or a psychiatric background a place to work and professional guidance. They represent artists whose work has been bought by renowned museums from all over the world and have their own outsider art academy. Here you can see the artists at work, visit regular exhibitions and attend events.

400 ROOT GALLERY

AT: HET ARCHIEF
Robert Fruin-
straat 52, 6th floor
West ⑥
www.root.gallery

You'll find Root Gallery in Het Archief, a creative breeding ground for artists and people working in the cultural field, located in the former city archive depot in Rotterdam West. The gallery seeks to represent a new generation of Dutch contemporary artists working in different disciplines and crossovers.

The 5 best places to see
STREET ART

---

401 READY2RUMBLE
Van Speykstraat 15
Centre West ①
ready2rumbl.nl

A graffiti artist from the age of 17, Ready2rumble draws inspiration from pop culture, American sports, and likes to draw animals and fast food. A lot of these subjects come together in this facade-filling mural in the Van Speykstraat. A bold and uplifting piece.

402 LASTPLAK
Corner of Baan /
Vasteland
Centre East ②

Lastplak is a painters' collective. For over 20 years they've been working on whatever surface they can find. You can see a lot of their brightly-coloured work around Rotterdam. There's a nice work at the corner of Baan and Vasteland. Check out their Facebook page for more locations and new work.

403 BIER EN BROOD
Ketelaarstraat
Centre East ②
bierenbrood.nl

Bier en Brood is an illustration duo from Rotterdam. Their work is featured in national newspapers, as well as on the streets. Some of their intricate black and white pieces are temporary, others stay around for a while, such as this piece on science on the side of an office building.

404 DAAN BOTLEK

Boomgaardsstraat 34
Centre East ②
cargocollective.com/
daanbotlek

Daan Botlek is a Rotterdam-based illustrator and artist and is known for his minimalistic figures showing up in strange places, on the window sills of dilapidated buildings for instance, or stepping through walls. Here, a single white man is scaling what seems like a collection of blue floating meteorites on the metal rear wall of the Kühne & Co architecture firm.

405 MELIKEPAINTING AND ROBERT ROST

Boomgaardsstraat 73
Centre East ②
melikepainting.com

The magpie in this mural is holding an engagement ring. Above the bird it says: 'Sam will you marry me?' Tymon, the artist behind Melikepainting, used this piece to ask his girlfriend to marry him. Of course she said yes. The part of the wall with the flying cranes is by Robert Rost.

403 BIER EN BROOD

The 5 best pieces of world class
ART IN PUBLIC SPACES

---

406 L'HOMME QUI MARCHE
AUGUSTE RODIN
Westersingel, opposite number 45
Centre West ①

Rodin's sculpture of a walking, naked man's legs and torso fit in with the image of Rotterdam as a worker's city, the municipality said when it bought the piece in 1960. However, it remained 'hidden' in the garden of Museum Boijmans Van Beuningen for some time, because a naked man might offend people. The sculpture is now on the sculpture terrace in Westersingel.

407 SANTA CLAUS
PAUL MCCARTHY
Eendrachtsplein (corner with Mauritsweg)
Centre West ①

Few artworks caused such a stir as Paul McCarthy's *Santa Claus*, which was purchased by the city in 2002. The reason: Santa's Christmas tree in fact looks more like a dildo. So a nickname was quickly introduced: *Kabouter* (dwarf) *Buttplug*. A permanent location was nevertheless found in Eendrachtsplein.

408 GLASS RELIEF
KAREL APPEL
AT: HOFPLEINTHEATER
Bentheimplein 13
North ③
+31 (0)10 243 50 50
jeugdtheaterhofplein.nl

When architect Hugo Maaskant was commissioned to design a new building for the technical school in the 1960s, he asked the famous artist Karel Appel to design the facade. Appel made an untitled artwork of stained glass and concrete covering an area of 6 by 24 metres. It's now the facade of Hofpleintheater and can be admired from both inside and outside.

409 WALL RELIEF NO.1
HENRY MOORE
Weena 762
Centre West ①

Rotterdam had to be rebuilt after World War II. To showcase the beauty of stones and bricks, the Dutch organisation of brick producers invited the English sculptor Henry Moore to decorate their office. Moore was inspired by the usage of bricks by the old Assyrians. His wall relief contains 16.000 bricks and was completed in 1955.

410 LOST LUGGAGE DEPOT
JEFF WALL
Wilhelminakade
South ⑤

The municipality invited Canadian artist Jeff Wall to make an artwork about the city, to celebrate its 650th anniversary in 1996. Wall decided to build it on Wilhelminapier, in front of Hotel New York, where millions of migrants boarded the ships of the Holland America Line. His iron sculpture shows the luggage of the migrants as they faced an insecure future in the new world.

5 of the most interesting
OLD AND NEW ARTISTS
from Rotterdam

---

411 DAAN ROOSEGAARDE
**Vierhavens-
straat 52-54
West ⑥
+31 (0)10 307 09 09
www.studio
roosegaarde.net**

A living wall, a smart highway or a dress that react to their surroundings: Daan Roosegaarde's (1979) innovative designs – or 'techno poetry' as he calls it – have won worldwide praise. The Rotterdam-based designer also designed a smog-free tower, which filters harmful particles out of the air to create clean urban bubbles. This award-winning design can be seen in several countries around the world.

412 KEES VAN DONGEN
**Aelbrechtskolk 15
West ⑥**

Kees van Dongen (1877-1968) was born in Delfshaven. As he was too poor to go to art school, he attended evening art classes, which were too rigid for his taste. He preferred to draw the sailors and prostitutes of the rougher neighbourhoods. At the age of 20, he moved to Paris. The wall of Aelbrechtskolk 15 shows a picture of Van Dongen painting in Delfshaven.

413 DORA DOLZ

's-Gravendijkwal / Mathenesserlaan
West ⑥

Warmth, plenty of colour and copious shapes characterised the sculptures of Dora Dolz (1941-2008). Born in Barcelona, she added a bit of sparkling colour to the dreary Dutch streets, which she called home since 1965. Her ceramic furniture can be found around Rotterdam. The two lounge chairs on this busy crossing invite you to sit down for a minute, as life rushes by.

414 JOEP VAN LIESHOUT

Keileweg 18
West ⑥
+31 (0)10 244 09 71
avlmundo.org

Artist, sculptor, architect, designer and innovator Joep van Lieshout (1963) is internationally renowned for his sculptures, installations and buildings. Recurring themes in his work are alienation from the environment, industrial power, consumerism and sex. His Atelier Van Lieshout is located in Keileweg, where you can visit a sculpture garden and temporary exhibitions.

415 WILLEM DE KOONING

Weena 103
Centre West ①

Painter and sculptor Willem de Kooning (1904-1997) was born at Zaagmolen, when Oude Noorden was still a working class area. While creating his sculptures, De Kooning wore three pairs of gloves, because he thought his hands were too small for a sculptor. In 1984, the municipality bought his *Seated Woman*. The sculpture is on display at Weena.

The 5 best
CULTURAL CENTRES

---

416 **WORM**
   Boomgaardsstraat 71
   Centre West ①
   +31 (0)10 476 78 32
   worm.org

You can never be sure what to expect at this cultural centre. An experimental Japanese cult film or a French police thriller? A provoking performance or exhibition? Or maybe a steamy hot dance night? After a performance, have a drink at neighbouring Wunderbar.

417 **ROODKAPJE**
   Delftseplein 39
   Centre West ①
   +31 (0)10 243 98 00
   roodkapje.org

The diverse programme of Roodkapje includes concerts and dance nights, exhibitions, performances and movies. The venue is located in the same building as Burgertrut, which serves great burgers.

418 **ARMINIUS**
   Museumpark 3
   Centre West ①
   +31 (0)10 436 38 00
   arminius.nl

What are the current literary trends? How should Rotterdam treat its art in public space and what's the future of Europe? These and many other topics are discussed at Arminius, a debate centre located in a late 19th-century church on the corner of Westersingel and Museumpark that focuses on topics like politics, art, science and society.

419 **ERASMUS PAVILION**

AT: ERASMUS
UNIVERSITEIT,
CAMPUS WOUDESTEIN
**Burgemeester
Oudlaan 350
Northeast** ④
+31 (0)10 408 97 42
erasmuspaviljoen.nl

Join students and academics at the lectures, debates, performances and concerts that are organised in the cultural centre on the university campus. The programme is diverse, with many events in English. The Erasmus Pavilion also has an affordable restaurant that received an award for its efforts in sustainability.

420 **V2_, INSTITUTE FOR THE UNSTABLE MEDIA**

**Eendrachtsstraat 10
Centre East** ②
+31 (0)10 206 72 72
v2.nl

Since its inception in 1981, artists, researchers, theorists and computer developers have used this centre for art, media and technology to share their findings and ideas. Debates, performances and other events (often in English) are organised at their home base just off Witte de Withstraat or in other locations throughout the city.

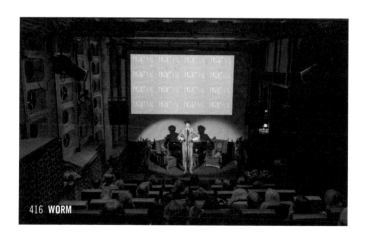

416 **WORM**

5 of the best
CULTURAL FESTIVALS

421 INTERNATIONAL FILM FESTIVAL ROTTERDAM
+31 (0)10 890 90 90
iffr.com

Twelve days, hundreds of documentaries, feature films, shorts and several hundreds of thousands of visitors and industry professionals. The International Film Festival Rotterdam is one of the largest film festivals in the world. The IFFR focuses on new work, but also organises themed exhibitions and retrospectives. It usually takes place in January/February.

422 MOTEL MOZAIQUE
+31 (0)10 413 79 18
motelmozaique.nl

A very creative music, arts and performance festival that's held every year in April. Schouwburgplein is the festival's beating heart, but performances are also organised in various surprising locations, turning the whole town upside down. There are several tours and fun activities as well. Motel Mozaique also organises concerts throughout the year.

423 NORTH SEA JAZZ FESTIVAL
northseajazz.com

Many legendary soul and jazz legends, such as Miles Davis, Dizzy Gillespie, James Brown, Sara Vaughan and Amy Winehouse, have given performances here over the years. Although the emphasis is on jazz, the festival is known for its wide range of musical styles reflected in more than 150 performances. The festival usually takes place in July.

424 ROTTERDAM ART WEEK
rotterdamartweek.info

Every February Rotterdam hosts a bustling art-filled week: Art Rotterdam, OBJECT Rotterdam (for design), as well as other fairs and expos throughout the city. The city's galleries, studios, cultural institutions and industrial sites also open their doors, showcasing the work of established and up-and-coming artists, making the Art Week an excellent indicator of what is happening in the art and design world.

425 SUMMER CARNIVAL
rotterdam unlimited.com/ zomercarnaval

What started out as a small Caribbean party in 1984 has grown into a full-fledged festival with the colourful street parade as its highlight. Imagine yourself at the Rio de Janeiro carnival, but with Rotterdam as backdrop. There are lots of parties, performances, plenty of tasty street food, drum battles and beauty contests. The Summer Carnival usually takes place at the end of July.

5 great
MUSICIANS
from Rotterdam

---

426 SEVDALIZA
sevdaliza.com

At the age of five she fled Iran with her family and ended up in the Netherlands. Sevdaliza lives in Rotterdam and released her first ep in 2015 – *The Suspended Kid*. She soon gained a following on both sides of the Atlantic with her ethereal mix of soulful r&b, synthpop and melodic house.

427 TRAMHAUS

With a DIY-ethic and youthful bravado, five-piece punk-outfit Tramhaus are rapidly conquering stages around Europe. Their electrifying live shows are a way to voice 'the despair of their generation', according to an interview.

428 KEVIN

The lyrics of rap artist Kevin are rife with odes to Rotterdam. Try *Langzaam* ('Slow', with references to the Feyenoord Stadium and Erasmus Bridge), *Gordelweg* (about the street with the same name) or *Havenstad* ('port city') which has the line "look at that skyline, worth the traffic jam". Kevin is part of urban label Rotterdam Airlines.

429 THE KIK
showcase.fm/thekik

A Dutch beat band founded in 2011 that seems to have stepped right out of the sixties. Their music is full of references to bands like The Beatles and The Monkees. Their contagious enthusiasm makes The Kik a much revered live band. Singer Dave von Raven regularly performs as a DJ as well.

430 BROEDERLIEFDE
broederliefde.com

This rap collective from Spangen (Rotterdam West) scored its first Youtube hit in 2012, with the song *Maluku*. A few years later, their album *Hard Work Pays Off 2* became the best-selling and most-streamed Dutch album. Their lyrics combine a mixture of Dutch, French, English, Arabic, Creole and other languages heard all over the city.

OCEANIUM AT ROTTERDAM ZOO

25 THINGS TO DO WITH CHILDREN

———

The 5 must sees at
ROTTERDAM ZOO

DIERGAARDE BLIJDORP
Blijdorplaan 8
North ③
+31 (0)10 443 14 95
diergaardeblijdorp.nl

431 GORILLA BOKITO

The most (in)famous inhabitant of Blijdorp is Bokito, the giant silverback gorilla who managed to jump over the canal and broke out of his pen in 2007 to grab a female admirer who visited him daily. Inside, you can watch Bokito and his family from a safe distance through little peeping holes.

432 AMAZONICA

As soon as you step into the balloon-like dome, you know you're in a rainforest. The fruity, heavy fragrance, the moist atmosphere, the luscious green plants... And butterflies everywhere. They perch silently high up in the leaves, or flutter down to eat from slices of fruit. The pupas come from Costa Rica and are hatched in Blijdorp.

432 AMAZONICA

433 POLAR BEARS

Polar bears in zoos can be a rather tragic affair, holed up in little pens, with no ice to be seen. In Blijdorp the polar bears have a lot of space and a terrific view of the city in this most recent extension of the zoo. Inside the building, watch the majestic grace of these bulky bears when swimming in the water.

434 BLACK AND RUFOUS ELEPHANT SHREW

This is one little creature that you have probably not seen before: a strange combination of a mouse on high legs with a trunk, brownish red in front and blackish blue in the back. It has the same ancestors as the elephant, but is not taller than a hand. Find it next to the crocodiles and near the meerkats in the Africa section.

435 OCEANIUM

No need to go scuba diving when you can walk through the Atlantic Ocean. In Blijdorp's Oceanium a tunnel winds its way through the aquarium. Watch sharks, rays and even sea turtles swim right over your head. Sit down and, for just a few minutes, imagine you're Jacques Cousteau…

The 5 best
PLAYGROUNDS

436 PLASWIJCKPARK
Ringdijk 20
North ①
+31 (0)10 418 18 36
plaswijckpark.nl

One day is probably not enough to visit all of Plaswijckpark. There are three different areas, or *wijcken*. The first is for playing and getting dirty, for cruising around in go-carts and pedal boats. The second is for strolling and having a picnic. And the third for admiring animals such as otters, black swans, wallabies, monkeys and lemurs.

437 SKATELAND
Piekstraat 45
South ⑤
+31 (0)10 290 98 90
skateland.nl

This is definitely the largest indoor skatepark (2600 square metres) in Rotterdam. Skateboarders, inline skaters and BMX-riders all flock to Skateland to practice their skills and tricks. There's a separate rink for smaller kids with small obstacles and a mini-ramp. They offer classes and regularly organise special events.

438 DE SPEELDERNIS

Roel Langerak-
weg 25-B
North ③
+31 (0)10 415 85 83
speeldernis.nl

No swings nor slides, at Speeldernis, you use nature as your playground. Climb trees, build huts, dams and rafts, learn how to make a fire and roast marshmallows or make popcorn. There's a separate, safer area for kids under six. Playing outside is more fun if you can get dirty, so be advised to wear old clothes.

439 DE ONTDEKHOEK

De Schuttersweg 76
Northeast ④
+31 (0)10 414 31 03
ontdekhoek.nl

Normally keeping children occupied for a few hours can be quite a challenge but not in Ontdekhoek (discover corner). At this interactive science centre kids find out how to develop photographs, how to build a dam, how to make chips from potatoes, how to make a sailboat or their own soap. And those are just a few of the options!

440 SPEELCENTRUM WEENA

Diergaardesingel 50
Centre West ①
+31 (0)10 414 48 90
speelcentrumweena.nl

A large playground in the centre of the city with grass, sand and water, so kids can play in a 'natural' environment. There is a castle to climb on, slides to glide off and a large sandpit to play and dig in. Open seven days a week, entry is free.

The 5 most
FUN MUSEUMS
for children

---

441 **VILLA ZEBRA**
Stieltjesstraat 21
South ⑤
+31 (0)10 241 17 17
villazebra.nl

An enticing art and do-it-yourself-museum for kids. The fun starts on arrival with an entrance filled with games and toys. There are separate, interactive play and art installations for the little ones between two and six. Kids can find out what it feels like to be an artist or a scientist in a lab, or they can create their own perfect pet with clay.

442 **KIDS TOUR IN DE KUIP**
FEYENOORD STADIUM
Van Zandvlietplein 1
South ⑤
+31 (0)10 492 94 55
dekuip.nl

Walk through the players' tunnel into Feyenoord stadium, have a seat next to the pitch and visit places where normally only the players and managers may go. The 90-minute tours are on Saturdays and Wednesday afternoons and include admission to the Feyenoord museum and some cool gadgets to take home.

441 **VILLA ZEBRA**

443 MINIWORLD ROTTERDAM

Weena 745
Centre West ①
+31 (0)10 240 05 01
miniworld
rotterdam.com

Miniworld Rotterdam is a fantastic way to see the whole of Rotterdam, and soon England and Scotland as well, in just a few hours. Watch the 27.000 inhabitants go about their day between miniature houses, along streets and in the harbour. Every 24 minutes the sun sets, night falls and twinkling lights go on. Wonder how this miniworld is made? Take a tour behind the scenes.

444 MARITIME MUSEUM

Leuvehaven 1
Centre East ②
+31 (0)10 413 26 80
maritiemmuseum.nl

Meet Professor Plons (splash) and his fellow passengers as they are preparing for a journey around the world by ship. They still need to do a lot before they can leave, so help them load the ship, raise the sails or cook a meal. This popular museum for children between the ages of 4 and 15 is also accessible for disabled children.

445 MARINIERSMUSEUM

Wijnhaven 7-13
Centre East ②
+31 (0)10 412 96 00
mariniersmuseum.nl

The marine corps was founded in 1665, when the Dutch Republic was at war with England. This museum tells visitors about its long history. A special family exhibition lets children experience what it is to be combat tracker: where should you look for traces and how can you interpret them?

5 GREAT AND CHILD-FRIENDLY RESTAURANTS

446 DUTCH DINER

Meent 20
Centre East ②
+31 (0)10 841 30 54

This is a perfect stop to recover from your explorations of Markthal or Binnenrotte market. Children can choose from a huge selection of pancakes or *poffertjes* (mini-pancakes), a Dutch treat. Not that keen on pancakes yourself? Don't worry, Dutch Diner also serves hamburgers, *satay* and fried eggs.

447 JUFFROUW VAN ZANTEN

2e Middelland-
straat 27
West ⑥
+31 (0)10 818 89 66
juffrouwvanzanten.com

A popular spot for morning coffees, laid-back brunches or a late afternoon lemonade or glass of wine. Juffrouw van Zanten has a spacious and leafy terrace, a kids menu and an inside play area for little ones. They also do a proper high tea or 'high lemonade' for kids.

448 BOSHUT DE BIG

Kralingseweg 20
Northeast ④
+31 (0)10 452 68 74
boshutdebig.nl

This pancake house is a fun stop during an afternoon near Kralingen Lake. The friendly wooden hut has been there for decades, and the recipe has stayed the same: thick old-fashioned Dutch pancakes served with bacon, apple or cheese, and lashings of syrup or sugar. Kids will love the tasty, messy pancakes and can get rid of their energy in the playground.

449 LA SALUTE

Bergse Dorpsstraat 65
North ③
+31 (0)10 422 11 22
lasalute.nl

This Italian restaurant has a separate play attic for kids, complete with babysitter. So leave the kids to play after they've finished their pizza or kid's menu, and take your time to enjoy a good, freshly prepared Italian meal. In summer, try to get a table on the vine-covered terrace.

450 OSTERIA VICINI

Kortekade 63-69
Northeast ④
+31 (0)10 890 05 55
vicinirotterdam.nl

This *osteria* in Kralingen is a family-friendly restaurant with a modern and bright interior. There's a play area for kids and they can colour the back of the menu while waiting for their spaghetti or pizza. For adults, there's additional choice in pasta dishes, risotto, meat or fish of the day and numerous veggie side dishes.

The 5 most lovely
SHOPS
for children

---

451 **DE KLEINE KAPITEIN**
   Botersloot 173
   Centre East ②
   +31 (0)10 412 47 50
   de-kleine-kapitein.nl

As children's bookstores go, they don't get much better than this. De Kleine Kapitein (the little captain) has a wide range of children's books, picture books, fantasy and comics, a fantastic array of book-related toys and gifts, as well as a play corner for the kids.

452 **VER VAN HIER**
   Kleiweg 69
   North ③
   +31 (0)10 845 13 36
   vervanhierrotterdam.nl

Ver van Hier (Far from here) combines a love of children's books with a love of coffee. While the children are reading, sit down for an excellent cup of joe and a slice of cake. There are regular events for the little ones, like writing workshops or handicraft afternoons. They have a well stocked English department.

453 **HUNNIE**
   Van Beethoven-
   singel 48
   North ③
   +31 (0)10 218 14 76
   hunnie.nl

Two floors packed with everything a small child could ever wish for: from wooden toys, games and dress-up clothes to books and dolls. This is the go-to shop in Hillegersberg if you're looking for a nice gift.

454 CARRABAS

Jonker Fransstraat 99
North ③
+31 (0)10 422 55 25
carrabasspeelgoed.nl

Two entrepreneurial mums who were unhappy with the selection of creative and sustainable toys on offer started Carrabas. It is now one of the largest toy stores in Rotterdam, selling lots of stuffed toys, board games, science experiments, magic sets, tricycles, doll houses and craft kits.

455 DE GEHEIME TUIN

Stadhoudersweg 87-D
North ③
+31 (0)10 229 12 60
kinderboekwinkel
degeheimetuin.nl

Named after the famous children's book *The Secret Garden* by Frances Hodgson Burnett, this is first and foremost a book-store, but you'll also find toys, games and some vintage interior items in this lovely shop. Owner Peggy Mulder has created a welcoming local hub for children and adults alike.

451 DE KLEINE KAPITEIN

HOTEL NEW YORK

20 PLACES TO SLEEP

The 5 most
LUXURIOUS
hotels

---

456 NHOW HOTEL

Wilhelminakade 137
South ⑤
+31 (0)10 206 76 00
nhow-rotterdam.com

Located in the striking new building by Rem Koolhaas on the south bank of the river. The bright rooms with floor to ceiling windows offer great views of the city. The rooms have glass encased bathrooms and Nespresso machines. There's an outside terrace, a fitness centre, espresso and a fabulously designed hotel bar.

457 SUITE HOTEL PINCOFFS

Stieltjesstraat 34
South ⑤
+31 (0)10 297 45 00
hotelpincoffs.nl

Politician and businessman Lodewijk Pincoffs (1827-1911) made the harbour in Feijenoord possible. But this great Rotterdammer also had a tendency to embellish the numbers in his books. When his fraud came to light, he fled to New York. This building used to be his office, now it's one of the finest boutique hotels in the city.

458 HOTEL NEW YORK

Koninginnenhoofd 1
South ⑤
+31 (0)10 439 05 55
hotelnewyork.com

Set in the former headquarters of the Holland America Line, the classy, nostalgic rooms have stunning views of the river and the city. Stay in one of the mint green towers, in the former caretaker's room, or in the director's offices. There's also a great restaurant with appetising seafood dishes, a stylish cocktail bar and a fabulous outside terrace.

459 CITIZENM HOTEL

Gelderseplein 50
Centre East ②
+31 (0)10 810 81 00
citizenm.com

Situated close to Blaak station, Markthal and the lively bar area of Oude Haven, this modern design hotel has a very welcoming and cosy lobby. The sleek rooms come with rain showers, LCD TVs and floor to ceiling windows. Food and drinks are available 24/7.

460 ROOM MATE BRUNO

Wilhelminakade 52
South ⑤
+31 (0)10 892 95 80
room-matehotels.com

Expect modern and neatly-designed colourful rooms in this four-floor boutique hotel in a former warehouse. It's conveniently located next to the Foodhallen where you'll find snacks and meals from around the world. Bruno serves breakfast from 7 am till noon and has a selection of working spaces and meeting rooms you can book.

5 of the
COSIEST B&Bs

461 ROOMS ON WATER

Wolfshoek 3
Centre East ②
+31 (0)6 120 437 09
roomsonwater.nl

The hold of this 1913 cargo ship has been transformed into a spacious bed and breakfast (six bedrooms in total, all with en-suite bathroom) and meeting room space. There's a lovely terrace on the deck. Owner Moniek takes good care of her guests and provides a wonderful breakfast buffet.

462 SIMONE BED AND BREAKFAST ROTTERDAM

Graaf Floris-
straat 82-B
Centre West ①
+31 (0)6 254 005 47
simonebedand
breakfast.com

Very centrally located on the beautiful and stately Graaf Florisstraat, this B&B offers two double bedrooms on the ground floor. Each room comes with its own bathroom. Host Simone will give you tips on where to go in Rotterdam.

463 B&B WALENBURG

Walenburgerweg 23
North ③
+31 (0)6 141 265 75

This B&B feels like your own *pied à terre* in Rotterdam. It's a nice apartment with your own kitchen and access to the garden, and is located within walking distance from the city's Central Station.

464 BED & BREAKFAST MARIA

Sint Agathastraat 25
North ③
+31 (0)6 452 401 16
bedbreakfastmaria.nl

After a long day of exploring Rotterdam, what's nicer than plopping down on your own terrace with a cold drink? Or better yet, starting your day with a coffee in the garden? Maria's offers both a private kitchen and cosy nook in the garden. Breakfast is served on demand.

465 ALBERTI B&B

Hugo Molenaar-
straat 49-A
West ⑥
+31 (0)6 179 065 85
alberti-bb.nl

Don't be fooled, that second b doesn't stand for breakfast but for free bikes at your disposal. There is coffee and tea in the two tastefully decorated rooms, as well as a fridge and microwave for preparing food. Better yet, step outside for breakfast. Alberti is located just west of the city centre, offering plenty of breakfast opportunities.

The 5 most
U N U S U A L
places to sleep

466 EUROMAST

Parkhaven 20
West ⑥
+31 (0)10 436 48 11
euromast.nl

Sleep under the stars in one of the most iconic spots of Rotterdam. The Euromast lookout tower has two luxurious suites, aptly named Heaven and Stars, with access to the highest balcony in town. Perfect for some romantic stargazing with a bottle of complementary champagne. Book at least three months ahead.

467 CULTURE CAMPSITE

Schiehavenweg 12
West ⑥
+31 (0)6 254 207 77
culturecampsite.com

A campsite and architectural exhibition in one. At Culture Campsite you can sleep in the most fantastical upcycled objects. Don't expect to see any tents or campers. Do expect a unique camping experience. Add the hot tub option to make your stay truly unforgettable.

468 WIKKELBOAT

Rijnhaven
South ⑤
Wijnhaven
Centre East ②
+31 (0)88 888 70 00
wikkelboat.nl

Sleep on the water in a cardboard house. These sturdy and sustainable 'wikkelboats' are made out of 24 layers of cardboard covered by a 'raincoat' to keep everything dry. Inside you'll find all the necessary amenities. The floating tiny houses have their own terrace and some even have a jacuzzi.

469 COCONDO

Kleinzand 6
Hoek van Holland
+31 (0)6 412 494 32
cocondo.nl

Local entrepreneur and bunker aficionado Peter de Krom transformed this former WWII-bunker with great attention to detail and a high standard of style and comfort. Lots of original details found their way into the modern interior. Profits are reinvested into maintaining and developing cultural heritage and nature.

470 DE VREEMDE VOGEL BUITENHOTEL

Van Baerlestraat 252
Vlaardingen
+31 (0)10 341 50 25
devreemdevogel.nl

A lovely outdoor, child friendly hotel with ten very unusual places to sleep. Imagine laying down in a space shuttle, spending the night in a fire truck, or hunkering down in an elevated old timer caravan. All rooms come with well-made beds, a healthy breakfast and a free bird concert. Vlaardingen is about 20 minutes by metro.

The 5 best
HOSTELS

471 ANI & HAAKIEN

Coolsestraat 47-49
Centre West ⓘ
+31 (0)6 252 169 03
anihaakien.nl

This must be the best rated hostel in Rotterdam. Ani & Haakien make you feel right at home. Bright and colourful rooms and a relaxed atmosphere typify this homely place away from home. There's free use of a kitchen, a living room and a garden. Oh, and there's also a big fluffy cat named Suzy.

472 KING KONG

Witte de With-
straat 74
Centre West ⓘ
+31 (0)10 818 87 78
kingkonghostel.com

King Kong is the place for backpackers and travellers who are looking for a little bit more than just a bunk bed. They offer free coffee and tea in the mornings, a luxury breakfast buffet, free movie nights, a luxury female dorm and rain showers.

473 SPARKS HOSTEL

Westersingel 1-A
Centre West ⓘ
+31 (0)10 436 30 80
sparkshostel.com

You couldn't possibly find a more centrally located hostel than Sparks, just a stone's throw away from Central Station and on the corner of vibrant West-Kruiskade. Rooms (dorms, privates and family rooms) are modern and colourfully decorated. There's a 24-hour reception.

474 ROOM

Van Vollenhoven-
straat 62
Centre West ①
+31 (0)10 282 72 77
roomrotterdam.nl

This monumental building has 17 private and dorm rooms styled in typically Dutch or Rotterdam themes. The hostel is located in the upscale Scheepvaartkwartier, close to the river and the Museumpark. There's a 24/7 reception, a hostel bar with happy hour, access to Wi-Fi and Netflix and free walking tours.

475 STAYOKAY ROTTERDAM

Overblaak 85-87
Centre East ②
+31 (0)10 436 57 63
stayokay.com/en/
hostel/rotterdam

Spend the night in one of Piet Blom's famous cube houses, located right in the city centre, near the pubs of Oude Haven and the restaurants and shops of Markthal. This hostel offers all the basic amenities, but be prepared to make your own bed and rent towels (or bring your own). They rent bikes as well.

471 ANI & HAAKIEN

#ANIHAAKIEN

THE PORT OF ROTTERDAM

25 WEEKEND ACTIVITIES

The 5 most beautiful spots at
KRALINGEN LAKE

---

476 VIEWPOINT OF THE LAKE

Kralingse Plas – North
Northeast ④

The north side of this artificial lake offers a fantastic view of Erasmus Bridge and the high rises of Rotterdam's skyline. There are some green fields and benches where you can sit down to enjoy the view, or go for a walk on the pier.

477 DE STER AND DE LELIE WINDMILLS

Plaszoom 324
Northeast ④
+31 (0)10 521 67 59
snuifmolens.nl

These 18th-and 19th-century windmills are the last ones in the country that are still used to grind spices and tobacco. The mills are open to visitors on Wednesdays, Thursdays and Saturdays. There's a little shop that sells cinnamon, nutmeg, pepper, tobacco and other products from the mill.

478 BOTANICAL GARDEN KRALINGEN

Kralingse Plaslaan 110
Northeast ④

This wildlife garden on the northern shore of Kralingsen Lake was created in the sixties. It combines several habitats, such as a bog, reeds, wet and dry grasslands and a new forest, and is home to a multitude of small land critters, birds and water animals. It's a very picturesque garden and a popular backdrop for wedding photos.

479 DE TUIN VAN DE VIER WINDSTREKEN

Plaszoom 354
Northeast ④
+31 (0)10 452 77 43
restaurantdetuin.nl

Have lunch, brunch, high tea or dinner with the city's skyline as a backdrop. This restaurant, which is located in a mansion from 1867, has a huge patio giving out onto the lake.

480 BEACH

Kralingse Plas – West
Northeast ④

Many Rotterdammers head to Kralingen Lake in summer time for a swim. There's a small beach on the west bank of the lake, in front of the De Kraal petting farm. A small section of the beach's north side is reserved for nudists.

478 BOTANICAL GARDEN KRALINGEN

The 5 best
BIKE TRAILS
to explore Rotterdam and its surroundings

---

481 EXPLORE THE NIEUWE MAAS

rotterdam.nl/vrije-tijd/ nieuwe-maasparcours

The Nieuwe Maas River really is the heart of the city. Follow its banks and explore the imposing architecture, the green parks and an uninhabited island, industrial sites, grand boulevards and most of all enjoy some stunning views. The entire trail, including bridges, tunnels and a ferry crossing is 28 kilometres long, but you can easily divide it up into smaller parts.

482 FOLLOW THE ROTTE

Follow the River Rotte, to which Rotterdam owes its name, northwards out of the city, starting from Noordplein all the way to the beautiful Rottemeren recreation area (a little over 12 kilometres). On your way there you'll pass old dike houses, windmills and green meadows. There are few cars along the way and lots of places to stop for a drink or to admire the view.

483 WAALHAVEN

Get a real feel for the port by cycling around Waalhaven. Take your bike through the Maastunnel and resurface on the southern bank of Nieuwe Maas. Bike on the left bank of the river towards Waalhaven. You can bike all around it until you reach the dry docks and the historic village of Heijplaat. Take the ferry back to the city centre from here.

484 HISTORIC DELFSHAVEN / SCHIEDAM / MAASSLUIS

This trail will take you from Eendrachtsplein westwards across Nieuwe Binnenweg into historic Delfshaven. From here, follow the signs to Schiedam and visit the modern art (Stedelijk Schiedam) or Jenever Museum. Return to Rotterdam or continue for another 13 km to the picturesque village of historic Maassluis. The whole trail is 20 km one way, with plenty of interesting stops along the way.

485 OVERSCHIE / MIDDEN DELFLAND / DELFT

From Hofplein bike along Schiekade and Schieweg to Rotterdam Airport (8,5 km). Admire the Rotterdam skyline from a distance amid the green fields of Midden Delfland. Here you can enjoy fantastic views of the city. Delft is another 6,5 km from here. Stop midway at cafe-restaurant Spazio at the airport (Malpensabaan 3) for a drink and some plane spotting.

5 exhilarating
DAY TRIPS

---

486 DORDRECHT
indordrecht.nl

Dordrecht has lots of museums, history and a bustling shopping district. It's just a 15-minute trip by train or you can also take the Waterbus that leaves from Erasmus Bridge. Hotel-restaurant Villa Augustus (Oranjelaan 7, *villa-augustus.nl*), about 2 kilometres from Dordrecht's city centre, is located in an old water tower and is surrounded by a beautiful garden. It is a fairy-like place to go for a bite.

487 SCHIEDAM
sdam.nl

The historic city centre of Schiedam has the highest wind mills in the country and was once an important *jenever* (gin) production centre. There's a Jenever Museum in a former distillery (Lange Haven 74) and the Stedelijk Museum (Hoogstraat 112) for contemporary art. Schiedam is just around the corner, take the tram, bus or metro.

488 DELFT
delft.com

Delft played an important part in the history of the Netherlands. In Museum Prinsenhof Delft, you can still see the holes left by the bullets that killed the 'father of the fatherland' William of Orange. The famous Delft Blue earthenware has been produced in Delft since the 17th century, when the Netherlands became a world trading centre thanks to the East India Company.

489 KINDERDIJK
kinderdijk.nl

The 19 mills of Kinderdijk are all listed as UNESCO World Heritage. It's best to visit them on foot. Take the Waterbus from Erasmus Bridge in Rotterdam or change ferries at Ridderkerk De Schans. Bus 489, leaving from Kralingse Zoom, also stops at Kinderdijk.

490 MAASSLUIS
ervaarmaassluis.nl

Maassluis has a small and picturesque historic centre and is just 20 minutes from Rotterdam by public transport. Its long history in fishing, shipping and ship towing is told in the National Towage Museum (located at Hoogstraat 1). On Saturday afternoons you can visit an old towing vessel called the Hudson in the harbour.

The 5 best places to
EXPLORE NATURE

—————

491 THE TEMPEL COUNTRY ESTATE
Delftweg 186
Overschie

The Tempel is an 18th-century estate with a 9-hectare beautifully landscaped park with ponds, forest and pastures that attract lots of birds and small mammals. Among the many old trees supposedly is also the oldest oak tree of Rotterdam with a circumference of more than 4 metres. The garden is 7,5 km northwest of Central Station.

492 BRIENENOORD ISLAND
Stadionweg /
Hoendiep entrance
South ⑤

This green paradise under Van Brienenoord Bridge was bought by Mr van Brienen around 1850 to establish a salmon fishery. In the 20th century it was used to produce metro tunnels. The 17 hectares are now a nature reserve and uninhabited except for the Scottish Highland cows that graze here. There are plenty of birds, insects and amphibians to be seen.

493 BIESBOSCH MUSEUMEILAND

Hilweg 2
Werkendam
+31 (0)18 350 40 09
*biesbosch
museumeiland.nl*

Covering 9000 hectares, this national park just south of Dordrecht is one of the largest in the country and one of the few places in Europe with freshwater tides. The park prides itself on its biodiversity and if you're lucky, you can spot beavers, sea eagles and kingfishers. Busses leave from Dordrecht's central station. Or take the Waterbus from Erasmus Bridge and change at Dordrecht's Merwekade.

494 TIENGEMETEN

VISITOR CENTRE:
Nieuwendijk 1
Tiengemeten

Tiengemeten is a tiny island with historical farmland and areas of (newly created) wilderness in Haringvliet. Spot a beaver, a spoonbill or even the majestic white tailed sea eagle on a walk around the island. You can explore the visitor centre and two museums. There's even an option to spend the night (check out *tinyparks.nl)*. The ferry leaves hourly from Nieuwendijk 1, Zuid-Beijerland.

495 KLEIN PROFIJT

Zalmpad 11
Oud Beijerland
+31 (0)186 621 888

In these 70 green hectares along Oude Maas, the tides still play an important role. Wear waterproof shoes and walk through willow forests, rugged grassland and reeds. Because of the rich feeding ground, plants and flowers flourish here and attract lots of birds. The Klein Profijt visitor centre (with a stunning terrace!) is about 20 kilometres south of Rotterdam and best reached by car or bike.

The 5 cosiest
BEACHES

---

496 'S-GRAVENZANDE BEACH
Nieuwlandsedijk
Slag Vlugtenburg /
's-Gravenzande

This 3-kilometre stretch of coastline is much less crowded than the well-known Hoek van Holland. It has three entrances and several attractive cafe-restaurants on the beach, like Elements and De Pit, where you can lounge in hammocks and eat wood oven pizza. Metro line B takes you directly from the city centre to Hoek van Holland."

497 ZEVENHUIZERPLAS
Siciliëboulevard
Nesselande

An immensely popular beach, visited by both Rotterdammers and families and youngsters from the surrounding villages, who like to swim here, play volleyball and barbecue. The beach is 800 metres wide and is flanked by a boulevard, giving you the feeling of visiting a seaside town. Nesselande is easily reached by metro (end of line B).

498 DE ESCH

Nesserdijk
Northeast ④

Come early if you want to claim a good spot at this small riverside beach with a great view of the southern part of Rotterdam's skyline. It's not a well-known spot and mostly frequented by locals. Get there with trams 21 or 24 (get off at the last stop).

499 QUARANTINE BEACH HEIJPLAAT

Quarantaineweg 1
South ⑤

Sick sailors who arrived in Rotterdam with a tropical disease were initially moved to the quarantine area of Heijplaat, a former site of the Rotterdam dry dock company. Behind this green area where artists now live in the former sick bays is a secluded natural sand beach. Follow the hand-painted signs and enjoy the beautiful view over the city. It is not safe to swim here.

500 ROCKANJE

rockanjeaanzee.com

The beach of Rockanje is a little farther abreast than the beaches at Hoek van Holland or Maasvlakte 2, but worth the effort. The wide, south-facing sandy beaches gently recede into the North Sea. Because of a series of sand banks there are not many waves, making this beach very child-friendly.

INDEX

COLOPHON

EDITING *and* COMPOSING — Saskia Naafs and Guido van Eijck

GRAPHIC DESIGN — Joke Gossé and doublebill.design

PHOTOGRAPHY — Tino van den Berg (autoexilio.com) —
p.190: Roel Hendrickx (roelh.zenfolio.com) — cover image: Katya Doms

COVER IMAGE — Depot Boijmans Van Beuningen (secret 287)
© artwork in front of the Depot: *Het Leven Verspillen Aan Jou (Wasting Life For You)*, 2021 by Pipilotti Rist. Courtesy of the artist, Hauser & Wirth and Luhring Augustine

The addresses in this book have been selected after thorough independent research by the authors, in collaboration with Luster Publishing. The selection is solely based on personal evaluation of the business by the authors. Nothing in this book was published in exchange for payment or benefits of any kind.

D/2023/12.005/1
ISBN 978 94 6058 3346
NUR 511, 510

© 2016 Luster, Antwerp
Fourth edition, January 2023 – Third reprint, January 2023
lusterpublishing.com – THE500HIDDENSECRETS.COM
info@lusterpublishing.com

Printed in Italy by Printer Trento.